MARCHING IN MONTGOMERY

MARCHING IN MONTGOMERY

A MEMOIR OF THE CIVIL
RIGHTS MOVEMENT

JOHN J. HARTMAN

International Psychoanalytic Books (IPBooks)
New York • http://www.IPBooks.net

Marching in Montgomery: A Memoir of the Civil Rights Movement

Published by IPBooks, Queens, NY
Online at: www.IPBooks.net

ISBN: 978-1-956864-63-2

In memory of Mr. Jimmie Lee Jackson, Rev. James Reeb, Mrs. Viola Liuzzo
and all of those who have given their lives in the struggle for
freedom, justice, and equality in the United States

Freedom is a constant struggle.
—an old saying

Contents

Chapter I   Saturday, March 13, 1963: Alabama Bound 1

Chapter II   The First March: Sunday, March 14, 1965:
Back to Front 25

Chapter III   The Second March: March 15, 1965:
All the Way with LBJ? 43

Chapter IV   The Third March: Tuesday, March 16,1965:
The Posse Attacks... 57

Chapter V   The Fourth March: Wednesday, March 17, 1965:
To the Sheriff 79

Chapter VI   March 19, 1965: Returning Home 87

Chapter VII   Re-Appraisal: 60 Years On: The White Backlash. 109

Acknowledgments.. 129

List of Photographs

Chapter I

Photo1: Malcolm X, 1962 23

Photo 2: Robert and Mabel Williams, Cuba, circa 1962 23

Photo 3: The beating of John Lewis, Selma Alabama,
March 7, 1965 24

Chapter II

Photo 4: Governor George C. Wallace of Alabama and
President Lyndon B. Johnson, circa 1965 40

Photo 5: Federal Judge Frank M. Johnson, circa 1965 41

Photo 6: Montgomery Police at High Street and
S. Jackson Avenue 41

Photo 7: James Forman, SNCC Executive Secretary
and Willie Ricks, Field Secretary, conferring with
police after the march is halted 42

Chapter III

Photo 8: SNCC workers leading songs at the Jackson
Avenue Baptist Church 54

Photo 9: Willie Ricks leading a non-violent workshop
at the Jackson Avenue Baptist Church 54

Photo10: John Lewis, SNCC Chairman, addressing
marchers outside of the Jackson Avenue Baptist Church .. 55

Photo 11: Marchers stopped by the Alabama State Patrol
on a night march 55

Photo 12: Clergy surrounded by the Alabama State Patrol
on the night march... 56

Photo 13: President Johnson addressing Congress on
voting rights while marchers are surrounded by the
Alabama State Patrol... 56

Chapter IV

Photo 14: Willie Ricks leading singing while march
is stopped by the Montgomery Police 72

Photo 15: The march to the state capitol resumes 72

Photo 16: The posse attacks marchers on horseback 73

Photo 17: A marcher is attacked by posse men 74

Photo 18: Injured marcher 74

Photo 19: Injured marcher 75

Photo 20: Injured marcher 75

Photo 21: James Forman and Rev. James Bevel of SCLC
try to calm the angry Marchers 76

Photo 22: Dr. Martin Luther King, Jr. of SCLC announces
that Judge Johnson Approved the Selma to
Montgomery march... 76

Photo 23: James Forman denounces the posse attack 77

Chapter V

Photo 24: The march to the Sheriff's Office begins
in solidarity 84

Photo 25: The clergy prepares for the march reading
SNCC's newspaper 84

Photo 26: Dr King announces the results of the meeting
with the Sheriff 85
Photo 27: Marchers listen to Dr. King and other speakers 85

Chapter VI

Photo 28: White Citizens Council sign on State
Highway 80 between Selma and Montgomery 104
Photo 29: The White counter-protest march, Montgomery,
March 18, 1965 104
Photo 30: White counter-protest march, Montgomery 105
Photo 31: White counter-protest march, Montgomery 105
Photo 32: White counter-protest march, Montgomery 106
Photo 33: White counter-protest march, Montgomery 106
Photo 34: White counter-protest march, Montgomery 107
Photo 35: White counter-protest march, Montgomery 107

Chapter VII

Photo 36: 50th anniversary of Bloody Sunday at the
Edmund Pettus Bridge, Selma, Alabama, 2015 128

Chapter I

Saturday, March 13, 1963:
Alabama Bound

"ALABAMA BOUND"

I'm Alabama bound,
I'm Alabama bound,
And if the train don't stop and turn around,
I'm Alabama bound.

The call went out from the headquarters of the Student Non-Violent Coordinating Committee (SNCC) on Raymond Street in Atlanta. Students in the North were needed urgently in Selma, Alabama to support demonstrators protesting the murder of 26-year-old Jimmie Lee Jackson during a night voter registration rally in Marion, Alabama. A trooper of the Alabama Highway Patrol had shot Jackson while he was protecting his mother and grandfather from a police officer beating on February 18, 1965, and he died a week later. On March 7, a march protesting Jackson's murder and in support of voting rights was broken up by the Highway Patrol and a mounted sheriff's posse as marchers led by John Lewis, Chairman of SNCC, and Reverend Hosea Williams of the Southern Christian Leadership Conference (SCLC) crossed the Edmund Pettus Bridge in Selma headed for Montgomery, the state capital. The marchers were tear-gassed and severely beaten. Lewis suffered a fractured skull. This event was well documented

1

by newspapers and magazines all over the world as well as national television throughout the United States. It became known as Bloody Sunday.

I faced a personal dilemma. Was I going to answer the call from SNCC and stand up for what I had come to believe was the most important issue facing my generation—the denial of human rights for the descendants of the enslaved in our country—or was I going to sit on the sidelines and let others carry on? It was a real struggle. I was a 22-year-old first-year graduate student in social psychology at the University of Michigan in Ann Arbor who had been awarded a Woodrow Wilson Fellowship for my first year of study. I had determined that I wished to become a college teacher rather than join the Civil Rights Movement full-time as my friend and classmate John Perdew had done. During the summers of 1963 and 1964 I had chosen to pursue my studies rather than to join SNCC in the South. I had missed Freedom Summer in Mississippi as my fellowship stipulated that I had to take French and Statistics in Ann Arbor that summer. Bloody Sunday represented a last straw for me. I decided to join about 50 University of Michigan students going to Selma to support SNCC's efforts to promote voting rights in Alabama. I gave little consideration to my classes, to possible consequences and repercussions, or to the possible dangers such a decision might involve.

This book is an account of that decision and of the events that followed. It is both a historical account and a personal memoir. I had no idea of the historical significance of the events that would unfold on the streets of Montgomery later that week. The perspective of almost 60 years provides some greater context and understanding of the significance of those events in Alabama in March of 1965.

As a psychologist I know full well that people do things for many different reasons. In retrospect this decision seems impulsive, even rash. It is also hard to put into words what I was feeling at the time. To the best of my understanding, my decision to go to Alabama made on the Saturday after Bloody Sunday was the product of many experiences over my life up to that point. The two most significant proximal events were the example of my classmate John Perdew who joined SNCC in the summer of 1963 and was arrested in Americus, Georgia and charged with insurrection against the state of Georgia which carried the death penalty. The other was the assassination of Malcolm X that occurred on February 21, only two weeks before Bloody Sunday. These were the immediate precipitants for my own decision to go South. However, there was more to my own story than just these two factors.

When I was accepted to attend Harvard College, I was informed of an opportunity to become part of a Freshman Seminar Program led by the anthropologist Dorothy Lee. Small seminars led by professors on a variety of topics were open to incoming freshmen. I signed up for Diplomatic History taught by Professor McGeorge Bundy as my first choice and Racial Housing Discrimination in Urban Areas led by Professor Richard Mann as my second choice. I did not get into Bundy's seminar but was accepted into the one on racial housing discrimination. Bundy was chosen to join President Kennedy's administration that Fall as National Security Advisor. He eventually became the architect of our increasing involvement in Vietnam under both Kennedy and Johnson.

Professor Mann, on the other hand was a social psychologist and Chair of the Boston chapter of the Congress on Racial Equality (CORE). The year-long seminar with a like-minded group of students, all White, focused around interviewing Black residents of Boston about their experiences with housing discrimination. Mann ran the class sessions like a self-analytic T-group in which we examined our own prejudices and racial attitudes. This class was a transformative experience, intellectually and emotionally, and gave me an interest in the social psychology of prejudice and ethnic conflict that has lasted a lifetime. At the same time the seminar promoted an activism that turned an intellectual interest into work for social betterment. The seminar thoroughly acquainted me with the depth and complexity of my own motives. Mann also served as a model of the kind of activist-scholar that I wished to become. Later he became a leader in the anti-Vietnam War Movement and met with McGeorge Bundy in the White House to urge him to end our involvement in Vietnam.

I was born in 1942, during World War II, in Detroit, Michigan, to middle-class Jewish parents. My father was a businessman, and my mother did not work outside the home. We lived in a mixed Jewish-Gentile neighborhood just south of Eight Mile Road, the dividing line between the city and the suburbs. In the summer of 1943, the city saw the worst racial violence in the history of the country. 34 people were killed, 433 were wounded, and most of the casualties were Blacks, killed or wounded by White police officers or the Michigan National Guard. I do not remember this, of course, but racial tensions had seeped into the culture of the city as I was growing up.

My mother employed women to help her out with housework and childcare after I was born. One of these women was Terri, a young Japanese-American woman, whose parents were sent to a detention camp in California for the duration of the war. Had my parents not employed her, I later learned, she would have been sent to the camp with her parents. I remember her very well and was sad when she left to go back to California at the end of the war when I was three. Another woman, Mattie, helped my mother with the washing and ironing. Mattie lived in an all-Black neighborhood on the other side of 8 Mile Road at Wyoming called Royal Oak Township. When

I went with my mother to drive her home, I noticed that Mattie's neighborhood did not have sidewalks, curbs, or even grass on the lawns like ours. It looked run down to me, and I did not understand why her neighborhood looked so different from ours. I did not like it and didn't think it was right somehow. I asked my mother about this, and she really did not provide any kind of acceptable answer. I was four. I later learned that Royal Oak Township had its own (black) police force and (all black) elementary school. The residents were recent immigrants from the South and poor. Royal Oak Township was essentially a segregated little town on the edge of Detroit! Its history goes back to the Underground Railroad as the enslaved escaped the South on the way to Canada across the Detroit River. Some of these former enslaved stayed in Detroit and were looking for a rural setting in which to live, and that became Royal Oak Township. It remained a segregated enclave and remains so to this day. As I got older, other maids from Alabama and Mississippi told my brother and me some of the details of how segregation worked in the South and how badly Black people were treated. This is how I learned about race and ethnicity in America at an early age. There were other things as well.

My best friend growing up was my next-door neighbor, Freddy. There were a large number of kids on our block who would meet on summer days at the vacant lot on the corner and play pretty much all day until the streetlights came on. The older kids taught the younger kids how to play the games. Freddy and I made up our own secret language and enjoyed radio programs on Saturday mornings. When we turned five, Freddy began catechism classes at his Roman Catholic parish. One day when we were playing, he informed me that the Jews killed Jesus who was G-d. Since I was a Jew, I was going to burn in Hell forever for killing Jesus. This was all news to me. I did not know what a Jew was or that I was one, but I did know what 'burn forever' meant. I went home crying to tell my mother the bad news. She comforted me and placed a call to Freddy's mother. Freddy and I remained friends after this, but we never talked theology again. That weekend my father, armed with a book I could not understand, began home schooling me on Judaism.

Another formative incident was the lynching of Emmett Till, a fourteen-year-old Black youth in Money, Mississippi in July of 1955. Till was accused of whistling at a White woman in her store. His murderers were acquitted of the crime by an all-White jury. I learned of this from *Life* and *Time* magazines that came in the mail to our house regularly. I was very interested in current affairs and read these magazines cover to cover. In this way I was able to follow the events that followed the Till murder. I read about the Montgomery Bus Boycott that started later in 1955 and the Brown v. Board of Education school desegregation case. These events began the Civil Rights Movement, and I was able to follow its development through my teen years. Emmett Till was 14 years old when he was killed, and I was 13. This made a big impression on me.

By February of 1960, my senior year in high school, the sit-ins, beginning in Greensboro, North Carolina, made civil rights the issue of the day for my generation. I happened to be in Greensboro that early spring for the annual southern trip for our school baseball team, playing the all-White Greensboro Senior High School. We stayed at a hotel downtown across from the Woolworth's that had been the scene of the sit-ins. We were instructed specifically by our coach not to take part in the demonstrations. There was a moratorium on the sit-ins during the time we were there, and so the issue was never engaged. By the time I got to college I was ready to get involved in the Civil Rights Movement myself.

In addition to the seminar on housing discrimination and the work with CORE, Malcolm X's first appearance at Harvard in March of 1961 at the Harvard Law School Forum had a big influence on me as well. Malcolm debated a popular Black NAACP lawyer-activist from Cambridge, Walter Carrington. At that time Malcolm X was the minister of Muhammed's Mosque #7 in New York City and national spokesman for the Nation of Islam (NOI) under the leadership of Elijah Muhammad. The debate took place in the venerable Sanders Theater. When Malcolm spoke, in front of the podium stood a phalanx of bodyguards known as the Fruit of Islam. They stood at attention, never changing expression. Malcolm advocated separation of the races and demanded land for that purpose. Carrington made the case for integration. My friends and I were impressed with Malcolm's eloquence and militancy even though we did not agree with his positions on separation. Malcolm X made a number of visits to Harvard as he came to Boston quite often to visit relatives and his then friend Louis X (later Louis Farrakhan), the minister of the Boston mosque. I met Malcolm on several of these visits and was initially surprised at his personal warmth and friendliness given what he had to say about White people being devils in his speeches.

The summer after my freshman year, I got a job working as a detached gang worker in the Jeffries housing project in downtown Detroit. I worked with a Black street-corner gang who called themselves the El Tigres after the local baseball team. My job was to integrate the group into the local recreation center by coaching them in slow-pitch softball. At other times I hung out on the street corner in a participant observer role much like that described in the social psychology ethnography called *Street Corner Society* by William F. Whyte that I had read in college.

This job concluded and I had a few free weeks before school started. My uncle thought it would do me good to see the Rocky Mountains that had inspired him as a young man. He gifted me money for a car trip to Colorado, and I was able to visit friends from college on the way. I was driving back, and between Denver and Omaha I heard on the radio that there had been a "racial disturbance" in Monroe, North Carolina and that Robert F. Williams was wanted for interstate flight in connection with this event. I was familiar with Williams from an article in the Jewish political journal, *Commentary,* written by Julien Mayfield. This was a periodical my father subscribed to, and I read it regularly in high school. Williams, a military veteran, began his civil rights activities in his hometown in the late 1950's. He became the head of the Monroe chapter of the NAACP and recruited members from the working class of Monroe. He first became nationally known through the so-called "Kissing Case." Some White and Black children in Monroe were playing together. A White 9-year-old girl kissed a Black boy of the same age. Her friend did the same with a 7-year-old Black boy. When the girls' parents found out, they had the boys arrested, and they were quickly convicted of "molestation" and sentenced to a state reformatory until they were 21. Williams protested this case all over the world through friends in left-wing circles. Eleanor Roosevelt even got involved. The governor of North Carolina, under pressure, eventually pardoned the boys, but they or their parents never received an apology or explanation from the state.

Williams had also organized a rifle club through the National Rifle Association. The Kissing Case had brought him a good deal of notoriety and a good deal of animosity from the White community. Monroe was about as far north as the Ku Klux Klan had any substantial support, and the Klan was in the habit of riding in caravans through the Black community of Monroe harassing its citizens and firing guns. Monroe had 12,000 white citizens and reportedly 7500 Klan members! In 1957, Williams' rifle club, now called the Black Guard, returned the fire of the Klan during an attack on the home of Dr. Albert Perry, the vice-chairman of the NAACP in Monroe. This confrontation ended the night-time caravans through the black community but not the harassment of Williams and his family. Williams had been evolving a more general plan for the Civil Rights Movement that Mayfield had written posed a challenge to the existing civil rights leadership, particularly the NAACP. In 1959, after a White man was acquitted of raping a Black woman in a Monroe hotel, Williams was quoted as saying that Blacks needed to "meet violence with violence." This statement brought Williams into conflict with the national NAACP and other leaders of the Civil Rights Movement that had sought to remain non-violent in protests and free of communist influence of any kind. It did not help Williams' cause that he had visited Cuba and had become an admirer of Fidel Castro and the Cuban revolution. Williams was never a member of any formal communist party, but he was definitely comfortable in the circles of the far left.

In the summer of 1961, "Freedom Riders" fanned out around the South to test the laws that forbade segregation in interstate transportation. Traveling in Black-White teams they were attacked, brutalized, and sometimes jailed in places like Anniston, Birmingham, and Montgomery, Alabama and McComb and Jackson Mississippi. Late in the summer when many of the riders were being released from Mississippi jails, two civil rights activists, Paul Brooks, a Freedom Rider, and James Forman, came to Monroe to visit Williams. They convinced Williams to give non-violent direct action a chance in Monroe. As the summer wound down and the Freedom riders were released from places like the notorious Mississippi State Penitentiary known as Parchman Farm, Williams invited a group of Black and

White riders to Monroe. This was to be a test of non-violence in a setting like Monroe. Seventeen riders accepted Williams' invitation and established a "Freedom House" and a local youth-led civil rights organization committed to non-violence.

Demonstrations were held around Monroe for a full week in late August, and tensions in the town were building. A Sunday demonstration at the courthouse square downtown brought large crowds of White people from as far away as South Carolina and a large Klan contingent. As the afternoon wore on it became clear that violence was brewing. Forman, elected picket captain that day, called for cabs from the Black community to come to return the picketers to the Black neighborhood called New Town. The only car to make it through the crowd was driven by Woodrow Wilson, a member of Williams' Black Guard. He was armed with a shotgun. When a White woman from England who had joined the protests attempted to enter Wilson's car, the crowd grew ugly. Police estimated that there were 15,000 White people in the courthouse square. Forman was hit in the head with a shotgun barrel and all of the picketers and Wilson were arrested. In the aftermath of all of this, a middle-aged White couple from a nearby town drove down Robert Williams's street, Boyte Street. They were stopped and threatened by a crowd of Blacks who had heard what had happened to the picketers downtown. There is disagreement about what happened next.

The local police, as well as state troopers and the FBI who had descended on Monroe, believed that Williams kidnapped the couple to hold them as hostages in exchange for the release of the civil rights demonstrators. Williams and his supporters asserted that Williams was protecting the couple from an angry crowd, and that they were detained for their own safety. In any case Williams and his wife and children along with Mae Mallory, a black nationalist supporter from

New York, left Monroe that night. The FBI issued an interstate flight alert and Williams, Mallory, two local young men, and a white Freedom Rider were charged with kidnapping.

When I heard the newsflash on my car radio, I made a decision which looking back is also hard to explain in words. Since I had plenty of time before school started and I had money left over from my trip, I thought it a good idea to go to Monroe and learn more about what had happened first-hand. This started out to be a research project on an interesting aspect of the Civil Rights Movement. I was excited at the prospect of an adventure perhaps more inspiring than Pike's Peak had been. Besides, I figured that Monroe would not be more dangerous than the Jeffries housing project where things had worked out well.

I left my car in Omaha and flew to Charlotte, North Carolina. When I landed in Charlotte, I approached a Black Sky Cap and told him I wanted to go to Monroe and asked for his help. He excused himself and made a phone call. He returned and told me that someone would meet me and take me to Monroe. I thought to myself that this was the Underground Railroad in reverse! Shortly, a middle-aged man in a dark suit and tie arrived in a Buick and introduced himself as Mr. Kelly Alexander. I later found out that he was the head of the NAACP for all of North Carolina, influential at the national level, and was opposed to Robert Williams in many ways. He had been part of the effort to censure Williams for his remarks about meeting violence with violence. Nonetheless, he was kind to me and graciously agreed to drive me to Monroe. On the way he kept asking me questions about Russia and China, trying to find out if I was a communist as well as questions about my motives. When it finally dawned on me what he was getting at, I told him straight out that I was not a communist, that I had read about Williams, was a member of the NAACP in Boston, and simply believed in the rights of all people to equal opportunity

11

in America. That seemed to satisfy him, and we spent the rest of the drive in amiable conversation. He felt that he could not be seen in the vicinity of Williams' house, so he took me to the office of Dr. Creft, an elderly physician who had taken care of the city's Black population for decades. I waited until Dr. Creft's practice finished for the day, and he drove me to Boyte Street and to Williams' house.

I was greeted initially as a breath of new life as everyone was quite discouraged because of Williams' departure and the events of Sunday. I also had to be checked out as there was a good deal of paranoia as well. I seemed to have passed the test and spent the rest of the week staying in Robert Williams' house. So much for the objective observer. I was welcomed as a participant.

I spent time with Jim Forman who had been released from jail, local men and women, and the Freedom Riders. While I was there, a cache of dynamite was found by the FBI in Williams' backyard, the phone was tapped, and state and local police patrols came down Boyte Street all night flashing lights into Williams' house. This made sleep difficult, and I spent the week decidedly on edge.

At one point in the week, Forman asked if anyone had any contacts with the press as he was anxious to get his version of events out. I volunteered that might be able to contact the *Detroit News,* as I was a classmate and friend of the son of the Chief Editor of the *News,* Martin Hayden. Mr. Hayden took my call, and I told him where I was and told him the Monroe story as I knew it. He was very interested and got a "re-write man" to put the story into readable form. Forman got on the phone and filled in some more details. That was my contribution, and I felt good about it. I was looking forward to seeing the article when I got home.

At the end of the week the demonstrators' trial on charges of inciting to riot was held in the courthouse. We integrated the visitors' section of the courthouse for the first time. The national civil rights groups wanted the Freedom Riders out of Monroe. William Kunstler, the civil rights attorney, came from New York and engineered a deal whereby the demonstrators would go free if they agreed not to demonstrate in Monroe for two years and would leave town immediately. Many of the Freedom Riders who had served time on Parchman Farm did not like this deal at all but reluctantly agreed. I paid the fines of Woodrow Wilson and the Freedom Rider Leroy Glenn Wright as a protest against the deal with money left over from my Rocky Mountain trip.

All of the Freedom Riders dispersed to different parts of the country, some by bus, some by rail. William Kunstler offered to drive me and several riders to Charlotte where he met with Harry Golden, the author and publisher of the *Carolina Israelite*, and brought us along. He dropped me off downtown after the meeting with Golden as my flight left later in the day. I spent the time collecting newspapers from the week's news about the events in Monroe. I stopped in a drug store to look for more newspapers. I noticed two White girls at the lunch counter who were looking at me and giggling. They were listening to Ray Charles which I thought at the time was a bit ironic. I was about to engage them in conversation when out of nowhere a White man emerged and told me to "leave those girls alone." He said he knew who I was, and that he was going to see to it that I left town. I asked him who he was, and he replied, "Let's just say I'm John Doe, good American citizen." Well, that was it for me. I gathered my newspapers, left the store, and hailed a cab to the airport. Up to this point it hadn't really felt that I was scared. I was scared now. I felt that this man in the drug store was part of the Ku Klux Klan and had followed Kunstler from Monroe and was now following me to make sure I left. I had had heard so much that week about the Klan influence in Monroe, that that was my conclusion. I now think that this was probably a Monroe policeman in plain clothes who was assigned to make sure all the Freedom Riders did leave town. Still, that would not necessarily mean he was not in the Klan.

When I got to the airport, I found a policeman and told him that I was being followed by the Klan out of Monroe and that I had been guaranteed police protection while in Charlotte. This was true as part of the deal that Kunstler had made, and I named the police official involved. The officer agreed and I set about getting an earlier flight out of Charlotte. The earliest was a flight to Atlanta, a layover, and connections to Omaha. At first, I thought that Atlanta might be worse than Charlotte but then agreed. They said that there was money due me as this was a cheaper flight so in order to get me the money, they would need my home address. I was suspicious and reluctant but finally agreed. News of all this spread around the airport and as I waited for the flight to Atlanta a crowd of Whites gathered to look at me. They seemed more curious than hostile, and the policeman I had first contacted stood as guard until my plane left. To make conversation, he offered that if he had met that Robert Williams, he would have shot him himself.

The whole event in Monroe was a debacle for the non-violent civil rights movement and perhaps also for Robert Williams and his family. Williams escaped North Carolina with Julien Mayfield. armed with a machine gun and made his way to Harlem, Toronto, and eventually to Havana, Cuba. Monroe remains a fascinating, if complicated, story, and gave me quite an education into many facets of the Civil Rights Movement in the South. There was the issue of the role of violence and self-defense, the role of black nationalism, and strategies of competing civil rights groups and interests.

I arrived home much more knowledgeable and quite charged up, ready to tell my parents how my trip out west had morphed into something else. However, I soon learned that my family was quite put out with me. First, they had no idea that I had gone to North Carolina under dangerous circumstances. Then my uncle was mad because I had used the money that he gave me for a purpose he had no use for. To top it off, my father told me that he had received a call from Martin Hayden asking if he knew where his son was. He did not. My father knew Hayden because the store that my father worked for did a great deal of advertising with the *Detroit News*. According to my father, Hayden received a phone call from the Detroit field office of the FBI asking him not to print the story that Forman and I had phoned in.

The exact reasons for this request are unclear, but Hayden made clear that national security was involved. Obviously, Williams' phone was tapped which did not fully register for me at the time. My trip to Monroe put myself at odds with my family for probably the first time in my life. I had been used to making my own decisions since I left home for college and did not anticipate that this one would have caused such trouble. I can see now that I put my father in a tough spot with Mr. Hayden, but at the time I was not deterred. I continued to make my own decisions and the rift was temporary. I never did get the partial refund on the airline ticket promised to me in Charlotte.

In February of 1962, I joined a large group of students at the request of the Maryland NAACP in Easton, Maryland. Easton was the county seat of Talbot County where Frederick Douglass was born enslaved. In those days the route between New York and Washington took drivers through the eastern shore of Maryland. Maryland's public accommodations were segregated. This was a source of international embarrassment as African diplomats driving from New

15

York to Washington were denied the right to eat at restaurants along the way. The Maryland NAACP organized an effort to challenge the segregation laws in Maryland with mass sit-ins at places of public accommodation. White students from the North were recruited for weekend demonstrations. When our contingent from Boston arrived in Easton, we were divided into a number of interracial pairs to go to diners and restaurants in Easton to be served. In my case, our team went to a diner and requested service. We were denied service, and the owner locked the door. We waited patiently on the steps. The police arrived and arrested us for trespass. I was booked, fingerprinted, and locked in a cell by myself. I later learned that Frederick Douglass had been incarcerated in the same cells. After a number of hours, I was bailed out by the NAACP and returned to school that night. I returned to Easton some weeks later for the trial. We were described by the prosecutor to the all-White jury as outside agitators and communists who had descended on the peaceful community of Easton" like a pack of dogs," and we were quickly convicted. I was released pending appeal. I returned again to school and did not think too much about this until I received a letter in the mail from Juanita Mitchell of the Maryland NAACP. She informed me that the Maryland Supreme Court had overturned my conviction and that segregation in public accommodations had thereby been ended in the State of Maryland. She thanked me for my participation. I later learned that my case had been attached to Bell v. Maryland, the major case outlawing segregation in public accommodations that was affirmed by the Supreme Court in 1964. These cases led to the Civil Rights Act of 1964 that outlawed discrimination in public accommodations nationally.

Thanks to the Freedom of Information Act, I learned that the FBI opened a file on me after my arrest in Easton. Surprisingly there was nothing in the file about my time in Monroe, however. I learned that the Freedom of Information Act does not cover the North Carolina State Bureau of Investigation involvement in civil rights events like Monroe.

Unbeknownst to me, my arrest had a big impact on one of my Harvard classmates, John Perdew. John lived in my dorm/house and was in my social psychology tutorial. After our junior year, John decided to work with SNCC in Georgia for the summer. He went first to Albany and then to Americus where the movement was strong. I had decided to stay in Cambridge that summer to work with Professor Mann on a social psychology study that was to be a book on small groups. Throughout that summer I was getting letters from John telling me about his experiences in Georgia and urging me to come down to join the fight. I felt torn. Toward the end of the summer, I got a letter from him from the county jail in Americus informing me that he had been jailed and charged with insurrection against the state of Georgia, a crime that carried the death penalty!

Around this time a friend from Boston University, Kay Smith, asked me if I wanted to go with her to the March on Washington. She had been helping to organize for the march with the Boston NAACP. I readily agreed. We took an all-night bus trip from South Station to Washington, DC. On our bus was Mary Peabody, the mother of the then Governor of Massachusetts, Endicott Peabody. She herself was arrested the next year in St. Augustine, Florida during a sit-in protesting segregation in public accommodations. When dawn broke, we were in Washington, and all we could see were buses. This was a very emotional moment for me. I could see that this was going to be a huge event and that we were not alone in believing that America should do more to end segregation and discrimination. This feeling of being part of something larger than myself was powerful, almost religious in nature. I teared up, somebody got out a guitar and we sang freedom songs until we made our way to the National Mall.

When we arrived in a sea of people from the buses, trains, and cars there were rumors that John Lewis was not going to be allowed to speak. As we were students, we were most anxious to hear what he had to say, feeling that being our age he was going to speak for us and do so in a militant way. I also wondered if he was going to mention that a SNCC worker, my friend John Perdew, was being held on a capital offense in a Georgia jail. We had a list of the speakers for the day, but we were most anxious about whether John Lewis was going to speak or not. It was not until much later that I learned about the controversy that surrounded his original speech that was accidently leaked the night before. There was a frantic effort to make the speech acceptable to the other speakers and organizations represented in the march. Apparently, Lewis and Jim Forman, who had now become Executive Secretary of SNCC, worked on the speech in the Lincoln Memorial almost up to the last minute. John Lewis finally did speak, and he delivered what we thought was a very strong speech. Sure enough, he mentioned the three civil rights workers being held in jail in Americus, Georgia. For me, this was the highlight of a historic day because of my personal connection to John Perdew. Dr. King's speech was yet to come. I had heard a version of King's speech that was delivered in Detroit earlier in the summer on a Motown record. Still, when he delivered it that day in Washington, it was stirring and inspirational, one of the great American speeches of all time. We got back on the bus for Boston, feeling that we had participated in something really historic for the country. Malcolm X later called the march the 'Farce on Washington,' but I felt he was wrong on that one.

Once school had started again, our dorm student government, raised $25,000 for Perdew's defense, a large sum in those days. He was eventually acquitted, as the Georgia law was ruled unconstitutional. He had, however, served four anxious and unpleasant months in jail. John dropped out of Harvard temporarily, continued his civil rights work in Georgia and married a Black civil rights colleague. He returned to Harvard to get his degree but remained in Georgia working for human rights the rest of his life.

As I was getting ready to graduate from college, Malcolm X was invited to address the Black students at Harvard who were in the process of formalizing an African American Students Association. I had many friends in this organization, but I was informed that being White I would be excluded from this meeting with Malcolm. The organizers must have felt somewhat badly about this exclusion as they proposed that I could have a private meeting with Malcolm before the formal meeting. I did not feel personally badly about the exclusion as I was by now familiar with the nationalistic impulse that prompted a desire for the freedom struggle, even at Harvard, to be a "Black thing." I did not agree with it, but I understood it. Of course, I jumped at the chance to meet Malcolm X one on one! We met in the Eliot House dining room just after dinner. His talk to the Black students was at 8 pm. A woman who was cleaning up the dinner dishes asked us if we wanted coffee. Malcolm was reported to have survived on coffee and he said, "Yes. I take mine black, just black." He said this looking straight at me with an intense glare. I had heard Malcolm speak enough and I had read enough interviews to know what he was getting at. I said, "I take mine with cream and sugar," looking straight back at him. He paused a few seconds, and then he burst out laughing. He knew that I knew that a dialogue on black nationalism versus integration had started. I must have passed another test as the rest of time went by in a most surprising way. If he remembered me at all, and I doubt that he did, when he came to talk at Harvard, I often asked him leading questions

19

about Robert Williams and the concept of armed self-defense. I later learned that one's attitude toward self-defense was a litmus test he had for White liberals. The night we met, Malcolm told me the gist of what he was going to tell the Black students. He had just returned from his *haj* trip to Mecca and had changed his outlook about race. He had split with his long-time mentor, Elijah Muhammad, and had left the Nation of Islam. He was casting about, for a new direction and was seeking supporters regardless of racial background. I was surprised by this development but was excited by the possibilities that this opened up. I mentioned a few possibilities of people I knew that might be avenues for connection. Our time was up, but Malcolm wanted to give me his home address and phone number so we could stay in touch. I found a piece of paper, and he jotted the contact information down. I left thrilled.

When I heard that Malcolm X was assassinated on Sunday February 21, 1965, I took the news personally. Because of the meeting I had with him just six months previous, I felt a sense of personal loss as well as a feeling of lost possibility.

I did not know at that time that Malcolm had actually met with SNCC workers in Selma in January. I was also filled with regret for not having followed up with Malcolm to offer something on the order of what we had discussed. I had gotten too busy with my graduate studies. When Bloody Sunday occurred two Sundays later, it just seemed that I needed to do something. The dilemma I thought I had solved by choosing an academic career was still with me. I was going to have to take a break to join SNCC in Selma if only for a short time. From my experiences in Monroe and my arrest in Easton I considered myself experienced in what going to Alabama might entail. Again, I thought Selma can't be as bad as Monroe.

I went down to the Student Activities Building and signed up to go to Selma and volunteered my car. It was then that I learned that we were going to Montgomery, Alabama where SNCC wished to set up a Second Front. We left on the Saturday after Bloody Sunday and with me were two White graduate students in social psychology, Rory O'Day and Jim Ledvinka, and three undergraduates, Norm Hatter, a Black Air Force veteran from Flint, Charles Tyler, a Black psychology major from Flint, and Hank Kauffmann, a White psychology major from Saginaw. Norm was engaged to Charles' sister, Phyllis. Hank brought his guitar. I brought two baseball bats, a large hunting knife, and a hatchet, the only weapons I owned. I had no desire to be a casualty nor a martyr. I was very mindful of how the three civil rights workers in Mississippi had died. They had initially been stopped by law enforcement officers in Neshoba County for a traffic violation and jailed. They were released but then murdered in a conspiracy between the Sherriff's office, the local police, and the White Knights of the Ku Klux Klan. Their bodies were hidden in an earthen dam owned by one of the conspirators. I was determined that this was not going to happen to us without resistance. I felt that my 1963 Dodge 330 was a match for any law enforcement vehicle we might have to outrun. I was of the belief at that time that non-violence was a powerful tactic, but that self-defense in a terrorist state was justified and necessary.

White skin privilege is a real thing. I knew full well that I was a child of privilege who received the best education that any American child could possibly hope for and a comfortable growing up. This did not disqualify me from wanting to join a movement to try to bring about changes in a society where white skin privilege had been used to oppress and demean. I was also a child of conscience who developed a sense of right and wrong thanks to my parents, my peer group friends, and some formative encounters in my growing up. It was unclear how the combination of 'white skin privilege' and a social conscience were going to play out in Alabama, but I was determined to participate in any case.

Before our departure there was a joke going around. A man up North wakes up from a startling dream that he tells his wife. "I had a dream last night that G-d told me to go to Alabama." His wife was worried because she had heard of all of the bad things that were happening to Black people there. She said, "I don't know if you should go. At least, did G-d say He would go with you?" "Well, no," the man replied, "But He did say he would go as far as Chattanooga!"

Additional Reading

Ray Arsenault (2006) (2007). *Freedom Riders: 1961 and the Struggle for Racial Justice.* New York: Oxford University Press.

James Forman (1972(1999). *The Making of Black Revolutionaries.* Seattle: University of Washington Press.

Manning Marable (2011). *Malcolm X: A Life of Reinvention.* New York: Viking.

Gunnar Myrdal (1944). *An American Dilemma: The Negro Problem and Modern Democracy.* New York: Harper and Brothers.

Timothy B. Tyson (1999). *Radio Free Dixie: Robert F. Williams and the Roots of Black Power.* Chapel Hill: University of North Carolina Press.

Curtis L. Williams and John W. Perdew and Rutha Harris (2006). *Education of a Harvard Guy.* Denver: Regis University

Robert F. Williams (1973). *Negroes with Guns.* Chicago: Third World Press.

C. Vann Woodward (1955). *The Strange Career of Jim Crow.* New York: Oxford University Press.

Malcolm X with Alex Haley (1964). *The Autobiography of Malcolm X.* New York: Grove Press.

Photo1: Malcolm X, 1962

Photo 2: Robert and Mabel Williams, Cuba, circa 1962

Photo 3: The beating of John Lewis, Selma Alabama, March 7, 1965

Chapter II

The First March,
Sunday, March 14, 1965:
Back to Front

Ain't gonna let nobody, lordy, turn me 'round
Turn me 'round, turn me 'round
Ain't gonna let nobody turn me 'round.
I'm gonna keep on a walkin', keep on a talkin',
Marching up to Freedom Land.

Ain't gonna let segregation turn me 'round,
Turn me 'round, turn me 'round.
Ain't gonna let segregation turn me 'round
I'm gonna keep on walkin', keep on talkin'
Marching up to Freedom Land.

Ain't gonna let George Wallace turn me 'round,
Turn me 'round, turn me 'round.
Ain't gonna let George Wallace turn me 'round.
I'm gonna keep on walkin', keep on talkin',
Marching up to Freedom Land.

Our trip southward was crowded, three in the front, three in the back of my two-door Dodge 330, but uneventful until we had to make a stop for gas and use the toilet somewhere in the mountains of Tennessee. We were opposed to using the segregated toilets, so we all used the toilet marked 'White Men.' This agitated the White gas station attendant who duly noted our "integrated" group and became more belligerent. I slapped the money down on his counter for the gas, did not wait for change, and made it to the car before anything worse happened.

We made it to Montgomery by mid-morning, tired but excited. It was cloudy and a little chilly but a welcome respite from the bitter Michigan winter. We were low on gas again and didn't know where our rendezvous point, Alabama State College, was located. I decided to stop at the nearest gas station to get directions and fill up. The experience in Tennessee seems not to have sunk in. According to the Civil Rights Act of 1964, we were supposed to be entitled to freedom of travel and public accommodations. Everyone jumped out of the car, happy to be able to move around. I filled up the tank and others went to use the toilet. Suddenly there was some sort of ruckus. The toilets were segregated. No one wanted to use segregated toilets. All of the customers in the station were White, and they began staring at us with what we came to understand was a 'Hate Stare.' We were an integrated group with Michigan license plates. We could be here for only one reason. We were carpet baggers, troublemakers, race traitors, outside communist agitators, or worse. If looks could kill, we would have all been lying dead on the cement of this gas station. I hurriedly paid, change was unnecessary again, and directions were out of the question. We jumped in the car and left.

We had driven a few blocks when I spotted a group of young Black women in a car bearing the decal of a traditionally Black sorority,

Alpha Kappa Alpha, the AKAs. They were the first collegiate Black sorority. I pulled up alongside the car, rolled down my window and asked the driver how to get to Alabama State. She took one look at the complexion of our entourage and said, "Follow us." We followed them for quite a while through twists and turns until we "arrived," and they waved good-byes. I didn't see anything that looked like college buildings, but I did see a long line of people on the sidewalk. I trusted that this was the right place, let everyone out, and went to park the car in the closest empty space I could find.

When I returned, I joined the long line of people on the sidewalk and at the very back of the line. My Michigan car-mates were nowhere to be seen. I could not see where the line began or what was happening at the other end. I learned from those closest to me in line that this was a line of march that began at an Alabama State building, and that SNCC was recruiting students for a march that afternoon. It was also rumored that the president of Alabama State had threatened to expel any student joining the SNCC protests. The rumor seemed plausible as Alabama State was funded by the state of Alabama, and it was plausible that Governor George Wallace was putting pressure on the Black college's president to expel marchers. It was also true that not everyone in the Black community agreed with the timing, tactics, and confrontational methods of SNCC. Hence the appellation of Uncle Tom, the Black man doing the White man's bidding, was used freely by those I spoke with in the line.

Alabama State College was founded in 1867 as a training school for recently freed enslaved. In 1965 its alumni included the jazz trumpeter Erskine Hawkins who wrote and performed 'Tuxedo Junction,' Rev Ralph David Abernathy who was Dr. Martin Luther King's second in command in the Southern Christian Leadership Conference, and Rev.

Fred Shuttlesworth who was the leader of the civil rights movement in Birmingham.

As I was chatting, I noticed two young Black men arriving and walking toward the front of the line. I took them to be construction workers because of their "hard hat" helmets and blue jean jackets. I thought it was a hopeful sign that students would be joined by working class men getting off from work on a Sunday.

This musing was interrupted by the noise of the line of people suddenly turning around. Someone said, "The march is starting." I stood still. I had just arrived. I didn't know exactly where I was let alone where I would be going.

"Get moving," someone yelled and so I started marching, leading hundreds of people to an unknown destination for unknown reasons only because I was the one who had parked the car! No one joined me at the head of the line and the sidewalk was plenty wide enough to have done so.

James Forman, whom I had known from Monroe, came running up, out of breath and angry. He was dressed in blue bib overalls, a white dressed shirt, and work boots. This outfit was a SNCC statement of solidarity with the tenant farmers and working-class Blacks SNCC was trying to register to vote in Alabama, Georgia, and Mississippi. "Hi, Jim," I offered, happy to see a familiar face. It had been almost four years since I had last seen him. "Who told you to march, Hartman?" he snarled. I wanted badly to point to some guy behind me but all I could muster was, "Do you want me to stop?" "Hell, no," he shot back, "You started it, so you can finish it!"

I had first met Forman in September of 1961 in the aftermath of the riot in Monroe, North Carolina as I have described. Born in Chicago but raised in poverty in Mississippi by his grandmother, Forman graduated from Roosevelt University in Chicago in three years, did graduate work at Boston University, and served in the Air Force. He had been working with tenant farmers in rural Tennessee before going to Monroe to meet with Robert Williams. Shortly after leaving Monroe, Forman took on the job as Executive Director of SNCC. He was older than most of the people in SNCC, was extremely intelligent, and had dedicated his life to the Movement.

As I walked up a hill into the second block, I could see a line of policemen blocking the sidewalk and part of the street ahead. They had light blue uniforms and held billy clubs across their chests. I later learned these were the Montgomery city police. I had seen billy clubs before, not up close to be sure, but I had seen them. These billy clubs were not thin batons but looked like sawed-off baseball bats, thick and heavy. I eventually learned that by marching we were violating a city ordinance banning all civil rights marches as well as a federal injunction against all marches while a federal judge ruled on the legality of Governor Wallace's banning of civil rights marches. It finally dawned on me that the men I had seen earlier were not construction workers but rather SNCC workers who were wearing hard hats to protect their heads in the event of an assault by the police as had occurred on Bloody Sunday, just one week ago. I had no hard hat, no hat at all, and no bat. My bat was in the car. As I got closer to the phalanx of police, I started looking for shelter should the police decide to violently break up the march. Since I was first in line, I was certain to get hit. I was looking for space between the houses where I might run. The thought occurred to me that my academic career might well come to end with the splatter of my brains on the sidewalks of Montgomery, Alabama. This was a great deal more than I had bargained for.

To this point we had no training, and no one had taken a pledge of non-violence. The bravado of self-defense had evaporated, and I was not thinking much about the philosophy of civil disobedience or non-violent resistance. I was more focused on how I was going to avoid getting my brains bashed in and running between houses was not out of the question.

As I got closer to the line of police, Forman re-appeared. I took this as a good sign, as direction was certainly needed. His presence reminded me of why we had come to Montgomery in the first place. I also thought back to what he had gone through in Monroe. This restored some of my courage, and I was determined to walk into the line of police with billy bats come what may. It didn't come to that, as Forman shouted for me to stop. This was about two feet from the police. While Forman and a police commander talked, I was looking straight at a Montgomery police officer who was about my age and wearing reflective sunglasses so I could not look him in the eyes. When I saw the movie, Cool Hand Luke, several years later, I thought of my own confrontation with the Montgomery police officer with the sunglasses. He was sweating even though it was overcast and not very hot. I was standing there wondering what we had gotten ourselves into. Forman was talking to the police official for what seemed like a very long time. What they had to say to each other for so long is still hard to imagine. Apparently, Forman had a permit to march left over from the previous week, and he may have argued that the permit was still good. But with the state ban and the federal injunction against marches I don't understand how that would have been very convincing. Finally, Forman and the police commander had a 'failure to communicate.' The march was called off, and the police dispersed as did the marchers.

I met up with our Michigan group, and I was relieved to have survived this situation with my brains still inside my skull. We found someone in SNCC who assigned us housing and told us where to meet the next day. We were assigned to a small, one floor house occupied by a young man, his wife, and young baby. We stayed there for the time we were in Montgomery until the last night when we had to move. But until that time, we slept on the floor of his house, ate with him, often with food provided by neighbors, played with the baby, and learned about the family's life in the segregated South.

The Black community generally welcomed us, housed us, fed us, and protected us during this tumultuous week. These were acts of generosity and courage in the face of a White community that was determined to preserve segregation and its way of life at all costs. The Montgomery Black community, of course, had been used to this kind of courageous sacrifice for some years beginning with the Montgomery bus boycott which began in 1955 with the leadership of E.D. Nixon, Fred Gray, Rosa Parks, Martin Luther King, Jr., and Ralph Abernathy. The boycott of the Montgomery bus system lasted more than a year and resulted in a Federal Court ruling that Montgomery's system of segregation in transportation was unconstitutional. In retaliation, Black churches were bombed, people were beaten, a man was lynched, and Dr. King's home was fired on by shotguns. By 1965, however, not much had changed in the segregation patterns in all areas of life in Montgomery, including the buses.

After we got settled that first night we went to a local bar and grill in the neighborhood of High Street and South Jackson Avenue, just north of Alabama State, for a beer and some relaxation. Forman was sitting at a table discussing something intently, probably strategy, with a small group of people who I did not recognize. It was unclear to myself, and my Michigan car mates what Forman's strategy might have been at that point.

Some blocks away at the state capitol building Governor George C. Wallace may also have been talking strategy. Wallace, who was completing his first term as governor, wanted to be President of the United States. Born in Barbour County in the southeast on the Georgia border, Wallace began his career as a Circuit Judge. In 1958, he ran for governor in the Democratic primary against the state attorney general, John Patterson, who had the support of the Ku Klux Klan. Wallace, regarded then as a moderate on race, received the endorsement of the NAACP before it was banned from the state entirely. Wallace lost by a wide margin. He later told a supporter that he lost because he was "outn*****ed," and he vowed never to be "outn*****ed" again.

He won the Democratic primary for governor in 1962, and he was elected with 96% of the (largely white) vote. When he took office in 1963, he stood where Jefferson Davis took the oath as President of the Confederate States of America. In his inaugural Wallace uttered his fighting words: "[S]egregation now, segregation tomorrow, and segregation forever!" As governor, he attempted to prevent the integration of the University of Alabama by standing the doorway of the building where two Black students were to register. This became known as the "Stand in the Schoolhouse Door." Wallace forced the federal government to enforce integration with Justice Department marshals and the threat of the 2nd Infantry Division.

Wallace sought to portray himself as the champion of states' rights against an oppressive federal government and tried to parlay this stance into national prominence. He announced that he would run for President against John Kennedy before the latter was assassinated and did enter the primaries against Lyndon Johnson in 1964. Very popular in the White South he also did well in primaries in Wisconsin, Indiana, and Maryland. In further political maneuvering, Wallace withdrew from the race for president, and the Alabama electors were unpledged which meant that President Johnson was removed from the ballot. Wallace then sought to switch parties if Barry Goldwater would make him his vice-presidential running mate. Goldwater declined. Johnson won the 1964 election in a landslide but lost in Alabama, Mississippi, Louisiana, Georgia, South Carolina, and Arizona.

In 1965 George Wallace was riding high. His strategy was clear. He opposed integration and the Civil Rights Movement in the most forceful way possible. His state police had shot and killed Jimmy Lee Jackson during a night voting rights march on February 18 in Marion, Alabama. For Wallace, violence against civil rights marchers was good politics. Black voter registration in Alabama was only 23% of those eligible. In Selma (Dallas County), it was 1%!

For President Johnson, Governor Wallace was a pain in his backside. Although he had just won a landslide victory, Johnson was worried about re-election. He was worried about losing the support of more of the South, and although he supported the 1964 civil rights bill, it did not have a voting rights provision. Johnson had wanted to go slow on this provision so as not to lose the whole South. He faced opposition from Wallace as well as rumblings of a challenge from Bobby Kennedy with whom he had never gotten along. The Deep South governors were a real problem for Johnson because they were Democrats who either supported Goldwater or a third-party candidate and were opposed to civil rights legislation of any kind. Johnson was seen by SNCC as reluctantly enforcing civil rights legislation and advocating a 'go-slow' attitude. However, on March 13, the day before we arrived in Montgomery, Wallace met with Johnson at the White House. Wallace had wanted to use the meeting as a forum to disparage the marchers and the Civil Rights Movement in general. But Johnson in a news conference after the meeting and with Wallace looking on, told reporters that he had told Wallace to declare his support for voting rights and to guarantee the right of assembly to all citizens. Wallace looked on impassively.

Johnson immediately ordered the Justice Department to begin to draft legislation for a voting rights bill.

That night, the Reverend Dr. Martin Luther King, Jr. was also probably considering his strategy. Unbeknownst to us, Dr. King had come to Montgomery on that Sunday night to testify before Federal Judge Frank Johnson who was ruling on the constitutionality of Governor Wallace's ban on civil rights marches. King was staying at the Ben Moore Hotel located on High and Jackson streets, the very corner where our march had been stopped that afternoon. The hotel was located very close to the parsonage where Dr. King and his family lived while he was pastor of the Dexter Avenue Baptist Church. John Lewis, the chairman of SNCC, was staying at the same hotel, because he was testifying before Judge Johnson as well.

King could not have been happy with Forman's defiance of Judge Johnson's temporary moratorium on marches. He and the Southern Christian Leadership Conference (SCLC) had come to Selma in January 1965 at the request of local activists like Amelia Boynton and J.L. Chestnut to help in a voter registration effort. The murder of Jimmy Lee Jackson had catalyzed the Selma movement, and Dr. King's involvement brought national attention to Selma. Reverend James Bevel, an associate of King's in SCLC, conceived the idea of a march from Selma to Montgomery to protest the killing of Jackson and to promote black voting rights in Alabama. Dr. King put out a call to all clergy in the United States to join him in Selma. Dr. King had originally decided to lead the march on March 7 but backed out due to credible reports of a plot on his life. This is how John Lewis came to lead the march along with Rev. Hosea Williams of SCLC. Lewis was marching on his own, as the march did not have the backing of SNCC as a whole. There had been a growing rift between Dr. King and SNCC over a number of issues with SNCC believing that Dr.

King was undermining SNCC's efforts in Selma and in the rural voter registration efforts in nearby Lowndes County.

On March 9, Dr. King had led a second march out of Brown Chapel AME church in Selma toward the Edmund Pettus Bridge and toward Montgomery. State police and county deputies waited on the other side of the bridge just as they had on Bloody Sunday. This time, Dr. King knelt in prayer and turned around the 2500 marchers and returned to Brown Chapel. This became known as Turnaround Tuesday, and it infuriated Forman and many of the SNCC activists. King had wanted to honor Judge Johnson's injunction until the constitutionality of the ban on civil rights demonstrations could be decided. Forman wanted to keep up the pressure.

On the same day, a White clergyman from Cambridge, Massachusetts, Reverend James Reeb who had answered Dr. King's call to come to Selma, was severely beaten by four white men after having dinner in Selma. The Black hospital did not have the facilities to treat his serious brain injury, and the White hospital refused to treat him at all. He was taken all the way to Birmingham for brain surgery, but his condition deteriorated, and he died on March 11.

Forman's strategy only became clear much later. He had decided to open a Second Front in Montgomery which angered King and Bevel. Demonstrations shifted to Montgomery after Turnaround Tuesday with some arrests. Forman sought to involve students from Tuskegee Institute and from Alabama State in these demonstrations. Dr. King may have had the feeling that SNCC was becoming more untrustworthy, as he had made informal agreements with President Johnson as well as Judge Johnson about demonstrations while the court was deliberating. Dr. King may well have felt that SNCC was becoming unreliable on the question of non-violence as well. The competition between these two groups for leadership of the voting rights movement in Alabama revealed some of the other divisive issues between them. SNCC was secular with factions that were religiously inspired and factions that were not. Forman declared himself an atheist. SCLC was led by ministers and was rooted in the Black church and devoted to a transformative non-violent approach to social change. SNCC was loosely organized and devoted to a group decision-making process that was often cumbersome and chaotic. SCLC's influence rested largely on King as a charismatic leader and was hierarchically organized from the top down with no female leadership in 1965. There was also only one White staff member. In 1965, SNCC was bi-racial and led mostly by males. There were influential females in the organization as well as a number of White field secretaries. Although King and Forman were almost the same age, SNCC was largely made up of students and adults in their twenties. SCLC was decidedly middle class in its overall orientation and appealed primarily to church goers whereas SNCC was seeking the support of the black masses, and in Alabama, the poor rural agricultural workers in places like Lowndes County. I believe at this point Dr. King had begun to trust SNCC less and less in private although ostensibly the two groups were working together in Selma. Dr. King's specific strategy was to wait for Judge Johnson's ruling before beginning new demonstrations. This was enacted on Turnaround Tuesday.

The man everyone was waiting on was Federal Judge Frank M. Johnson of the Middle District of Alabama. Judge Johnson was from Winston County in the hilly northwest area of Alabama. This area had no cotton, few enslaved, and was a Unionist stronghold during the Civil War. Judge Johnson's family had been Republicans and were opposed to the segregationist position of the Alabama Democratic Party. President Eisenhower appointed him to the Federal bench in

1955. He had also been a classmate of Governor George Wallace at the University of Alabama Law School.

In 1955, when Rosa Parks refused to give up her seat to a White man on a Montgomery bus, the subsequent bus boycott led to a number of court cases challenging the system of segregation in Alabama. One of these cases, *Browder v. Gayle,* led to Judge Johnson's ruling that segregation in public facilities was unconstitutional. He was also involved in the case of *Lee v. Macon County Board of Education* that led to the nation's first state-wide school desegregation order in 1963. Crosses were burned on his lawn after these decisions, and in 1967 his parents' home was bombed.

From these rulings, King had reason to believe that Judge Johnson would side with the marchers and against his old classmate over the Selma demonstrations. However, the ruling was taking some time, too much time for Forman and some of the SNCC workers.

Forman's ostensible strategy was quite clear. He wanted to keep the pressure on Governor Wallace through demonstrations and continue to radicalize students and others to join SNCC in a mass movement for voting rights and economic justice. Forman believed that involvement in mass demonstrations was a way to develop commitment to the cause of social change. He was committed to non-violent direct action as a tactic, but not as a goal in itself or a way of life. During the week of March 8, he had contacted a group of students from nearby Tuskegee Institute. He wished to radicalize them in demonstrations utilizing as headquarters the Dexter Avenue Baptist Church where Dr. King had been pastor. At the end of that week, Forman had sent out the call for Northern students to come to Montgomery rather than to Selma. His plan was for even larger demonstrations for the week of March 15. That is the strategy that we had joined without knowing initially all of the complex maneuverings that had been taking place.

There was another aspect to Forman's strategy of using Northern students that I would like to suggest. Unfortunately, it was the White segregationist violent responses that got the most attention from the media and from the federal government. The failure of Dr. King's involvement in the Albany (Georgia) Movement was the refusal of Albany officials to overreact to Dr. King and the demonstrators. This was a strategy devised by the Albany police chief Laurie Pritchett, and it worked against the civil rights protesters. However, in Birmingham, Alabama the arrogant overreactions of the public safety commissioner Eugene (Bull) Conner with the use of police dogs and high-pressure fire hoses on Black children was documented by television and print reporters and led to condemnation of the segregationists from around the world. Forman was in Birmingham during this so-called Children's March in 1963 and was a close observer of this tactic's originator, Reverend Wyatt T. Walker. Forman had first met Walker in Monroe when Walker had represented the SCLC in trying to extricate the Freedom Riders from their involvement with Robert Williams. A large White man had repeatedly attacked Walker as he attempted to climb the steps of the Union County Courthouse in Monroe, mistaking him for one of Williams' supporters.

Malcolm Gladwell in his book, *David and Goliath: Underdogs, Misfits, and the Art of Battling Giants,* devotes a chapter to Reverend Walker and the strategy of the Birmingham Children's March. Gladwell likens Walker's strategy to that of the trickster in African-American folktales, the most famous of which may be the contests between Brer Rabbit and Brer Fox and the story of the tar baby. This was also a favorite story of mine as a child, and I was read this story over and over again by my parents. Brer Fox had made a likeness of a baby out of tar to trap Brer Rabbit. He succeeded in capturing him, but Brer Rabbit implored the fox not to throw him in the briar patch. The rabbit implied that this was the worst thing the fox could do to him. Finally, Brer Fox flung Brer Rabbit into the briar patch. Now the briar patch was where Brer Rabbit was most familiar, and he used the briars to extricate himself from the tar and escape. In Birmingham, Wyatt Walker was Brer Rabbit and Bull Connor was Brer Fox. When Connor ordered the fire hoses and the police dogs, as vicious and dangerous as this was, Wyatt Walker had sprung a trap. Bull Connor had fallen for the trap and earned the disapproval of most of the world. I believe James Foreman learned this tactic from this experience in Birmingham. In Montgomery he had White and Black college students in significant numbers to lure the fox into violence. Would the advantage of white skin privilege play any part in the drama that playing out in the street of Alabama?

Now as we were having our meal in the bar and grill on South Jackson Street, we knew nothing of these strategies and behind-the-scenes machinations.

We knew nothing of the meeting between President Johnson and Governor Wallace. We knew nothing about Judge Johnson's deliberations or even that demonstrations were banned by local, state, and Federal authorities. There was Wallace versus Johnson with the presidency at stake. There was Forman versus King with the leadership of the civil rights movement at stake. And there was Forman versus Alabama law enforcement with our well-being at stake. The abortive march that I "led" actually violated Gov. Wallace's ban, the city of Montgomery's ban, and Judge Johnson's federal injunction. None of this really mattered to us. We were volunteer foot soldiers willing to do what we were told to do, and Forman was our leader.

Additional Reading

Jack Bass (1992). *Taming the Storm: The Life and Times of Frank M. Johnson, Jr. and the South's Fight Over Civil Rights.* New York: Doubleday.

Clayborne Carson (1981). *In Struggle: SNCC and the Black Wakening of the 1960's.* Cambridge, MA: Harvard University Press.

James Forman (1972). *The Making of Black Revolutionaries.* Seattle: University of Washington.

Malcolm Gladwell (2015). *David and Goliath: Underdogs, Misfits, and the Art of Battling Giants.* Boston: Back Bay Books.

John Lewis (1998). *Walking with the Wind: A Memoir of the Movement.* New York: Simon and Schuster.

Howard Zinn (1964). *SNCC: The New Abolitionists.* Boston Beacon Press.

Photo 4: Governor George C. Wallace of Alabama and President Lyndon B. Johnson, circa 1965

Photo 5: Federal Judge Frank M. Johnson, circa 1965

Photo 6: Montgomery Police at High Street and S. Jackson Avenue
(Image from the Glen Pearcy Collection, courtesy of the American Folklife Center,
Library of Congress, afc 2012040_040_38)

Photo 7: James Forman, SNCC Executive Secretary and Willie Ricks,
Field Secretary, conferring with police after the march is halted
(Image from the Glen Pearcy Collection, courtesy of the American Folklife Center,
Library of Congress, afc 2012040_040_15)

Chapter III

The Second March: March 15, 1965: All the Way with LBJ?

I'm gonna do what the Spirit say do.
I'm gonna march when the Spirit say march
When the Spirit say march, O Lord,
I'm gonna march when the Spirit say march.

I'm gonna do what the Sprit say do.
I'm gonna fight when the spirit say fight
When the Spirit say fight, O Lord,
I'm gonna fight when the Sprit say fight.

I'm gonna do when the Sprit say do.
I'm goin' to jail when the Sprit say jail.
When the Sprit say jail, O Lord,
I'm goin' to jail when the Spirit say jail.

— African-American spiritual

Our second day in Montgomery began as an organizational day. We assembled at a vacant church building, Jackson Avenue Baptist Church, in the neighborhood near Alabama State. Willie Ricks, a SNCC field secretary who had come over from Lowndes County to help organize the demonstrations in Montgomery, greeted us. Bill Ware and Bill Hall who were Mississippi SNCC workers joined him. Ricks was born and raised in Chattanooga and had joined SNCC after meeting Forman. He worked with my classmate John Perdew in Americus, Georgia and participated in Freedom Summer in Mississippi. He was known in the Movement for his fiery oratory and was the one who coined the slogan, 'Black Power.'

The building was too small to hold all the people who had gathered on that Monday. Workshops had to be held both inside and outside the building. By this time the Alabama State and Tuskegee students had been joined by many students from the North. Judging by signs that the students fashioned for the marches, UMass, Antioch, Harvard, Georgetown, Pittsburg as well as smaller colleges like Mt. Mercy and Juniata sent students. We all took part in a crash course on non-violent direct action, SNCC-style. The history of SNCC, its philosophy and approach, how to behave in a demonstration were all covered in some fashion. Ricks was quick to point out that we were having to use this vacant building because the SCLC was putting pressure on local ministers not to cooperate with SNCC. In the previous week, SNCC led demonstrations out of the Dexter Avenue Baptist Church, Dr. King's church when he was in Montgomery, but was not allowed to do so this week. The animosity between SNCC and SCLC was clear and the differences in philosophy and tactics were clearly spelled out. Dr. King wanted to abide by Judge Johnson's moratorium on demonstrations, and SNCC did not. We had inadvertently chosen a side in that argument when we marched the day before.

One order of business was the election of a student to act as secretary of the assembled group. Steve Schwartz, a White undergrad from the University of Michigan, was nominated by Ricks and elected.

SNCC was a very egalitarian organization. Although it had an elected Executive Secretary, Foreman, and an elected Chairman, John Lewis, the organization was not hierarchically organized.

The field secretaries working in communities had a great deal of autonomy as did each individual member to act according to his or her own conscience and best judgment. The election of a student to help organize the demonstrations was part of the SNCC ethic to distribute leadership and empower all of the participants.

SNCC had been the idea of Ella Baker, a dynamic woman, who in 1960 was the only woman in the SCLC. When the lunch counter sit-ins organized by Black college students began to spring up in North Carolina and elsewhere, she saw a need for an organizing body to coordinate these spontaneous demonstrations into a social movement. SNCC evolved out of a conference organized by Baker at Shaw University in Raleigh, North Carolina in April of 1960. After the Freedom Rides even more Black students in the South became involved, and SNCC offered an organizing framework for their protest. The egalitarian sprit of its founding maintained itself in its organizational structure that had its distinct disadvantages as well. It was hard to get a consensus on almost all substantive issues which made for an unwieldy decision-making process. When Forman agreed to become Executive Secretary, he brought some organizational and practical guidance to a sometimes chaotic process.

In our crash course, Ricks made no bones about the differences between SCLC and SNCC's approach to the current drive for voting rights in Alabama.

King was criticized for his charismatic leadership style and the hierarchical top-down organization of SCLC. There was clearly a generational issue here. Ricks was 22 and Dr. King was 36. Interestingly Forman was King's age, but he identified with the students. There was also the issue of class. SCLC was church-based and middle-class in its values. SCLC member most often wore dark suits and ties to demonstrations. SNCC workers wore denim bib overalls and work boots in solidarity with poor and working-class people they were hoping would join the Movement. SCLC was religious not only in its membership but in its commitment to non-violent protest as a redemptive experience for all in a distinctly Christian tradition. SNCC had always had a faction of its leadership, particularly John Lewis, who shared this commitment to non-violence as a means of a larger Christian redemption for protester and segregationist alike. The Rev. James Lawson of Nashville, an early influence on the Nashville Movement and the Freedom Rides, had heavily influenced this faction. There were others in SNCC who were much less religious and committed to non-violence as a tactic rather than a philosophy of life. SNCC was secular but with distinct factions representing different orientations toward non-violence, redemptive Christian philosophy, and political goals.

As far as political goals were concerned, SNCC accepted a variety of ideologies and approaches into its ranks and adopted no one over-arching political philosophy. But SNCC was, by 1965, an important part of the amorphous New Left with a distrust of traditional political strategies. The March on Washington for Jobs and Freedom held in August of 1963, show-cased a coalition of the five major civil rights organizations (including SNCC) and organized labor and Catholic, Protestant, and Jewish leadership. This coalition proved to be a powerful force in the 1964 presidential election that was a landslide victory for Lyndon B. Johnson and the Democratic Party. SNCC had always been an uneasy partner in this coalition and was not in any way an arm of the Democratic Party. Some other participants, including the Archbishop of Washington, Cardinal Doyle, deemed the speech that John Lewis was to give at the March on Washington unacceptable.

The speech was very critical of the Kennedy Administration for not moving on promised civil rights legislation and for not protecting civil rights workers in the South. He used words like 'revolution' and 'the black masses' and vowed to march through the South like Sherman but non-violently. Lewis was urged to modify his speech and many hours were spent on the morning of the march, with Forman, going over the speech in order to make it acceptable to the coalition without selling out the principles of SNCC.

While SNCC did not have a distinct political philosophy, it tended not to trust compromise, half-measures, and empty good will on the part of potential allies.

In 1965 while there was no articulated vision of what revolutionary change would be like, most SNCC workers were vaguely socialist and were seeking to empower poor black people in the South. With the passage of the 1964 Civil Rights Act, SNCC was moving toward more fundamental change in the political-economic structure of the South. They had been doing this since 1963 by trying to build grass-roots organizations of poor black people in Mississippi and Southwest Georgia primarily.

Freedom Summer in 1964 was a crucial step in building these structures in Mississippi.

It was also part of SNCC's way of working not to exclude anyone or any organization that wanted to further the goals of SNCC. This meant that SNCC would take help from communists or former communists, and organizations like the Southern Conference Educational Fund that were deemed to be communist fronts by segregationists or the House Un-American Activities Committee (HUAC). It also meant that they would take help from the Lawyers Guild, a group long associated with radical causes. This put SNCC on a collision course with SCLC that had its own problems with accepting help from ex-communists and with organized labor, especially Walter Reuther, who had fought to purge his ranks of communists for decades. J. Edgar Hoover, the Director of the FBI, firmly believed that the civil rights movement was thoroughly infiltrated by communists, and segregationists thought they had confirmation of his beliefs in the case of SNCC. Hoover was wrong, dead wrong about SNCC. There was no ideology that was going to dominate the band of brothers and sisters that was SNCC. Forman believed that the building of a social movement stemmed from participation in the act of protest. This is why we were marching and also why he let me proceed with "my" march on our first day. The way to learn about social change was to see some action, to march, to protest, even get beaten up. That he believed was the best education, not ideology.

We also spent some time in this workshop learning freedom songs. These songs were variations on songs from church whose lyrics were adapted for the civil rights movement. Singing was a very important part of the movement and played a role in the marches themselves. Not only did the singing help to create a feeling of solidarity in the group but it also conveyed the militant protest aspect of the demonstration. It put the law enforcement agents in the morally difficult position of stopping and beating peaceful citizens protesting through songs with a religiously-inspired message. For me, the singing also seemed to be an outlet for the anxiety I felt in the marches that had an uncertain outcome.

As we listened to Willie Ricks tell us about SNCC and non-violent direct action, unbeknownst to us, SNCC was undergoing change within its own formation.

There were factions within SNCC that were beginning to lose faith in non-violence even as a tactic and becoming more uncomfortable with SNCC as an interracial cadre building an egalitarian community. Willie Ricks would eventually come to represent this cleavage in thinking as he was the one who popularized the slogan 'Black Power.' This slogan was a shortened version of the goal of empowering poor black people that had always been SNCC's goal. However, Black Power came to connote anti-white, violent methods to achieve social change. None of this was in evidence during our time in Montgomery. Ricks treated us like brothers in struggle against an unjust system and our tactics were strictly non-violent.

The highlight of this day of orientation was a short speech by Chairman John Lewis. Lewis was just out of the hospital. He had sustained a fractured skull from the beating at the hands of an Alabama State patrolman. I do not remember much about the speech as we were far back in the large crowd of students. But his very presence tells you all you need to know about this man of great persistence and courage. We also heard from Reverend James Bevel of SCLC who was the one who came up with the idea of a march from Selma to Montgomery. Bevel was known for wearing a yarmulke on his bald head and for marrying Diane Nash, reputed to be the prettiest woman in the Civil Rights Movement. He, Nash, and Bernard Lafayette and his then wife, Colia, led SNCC's efforts in organizing for voting rights in Selma beginning in 1963. By 1965 Bevel and Nash were members of SCLC and supported King's more cautious approach. Bevel became more distrustful of SNCC and was concerned about Forman's demonstrations in Montgomery turning violent.

Toward the end of the afternoon, Ricks deemed us well enough prepared and we planned to meet in the early evening for a night march. Our goal was to reach the State Capitol building to protest the killing of Jimmie Lee Jackson to Governor Wallace. Perhaps Forman felt that the authorities would not expect a night march.

The idea of a night march seemed a dangerous idea. Not only can bad things happen under the cover of darkness, but the White men of Montgomery were home from work and could pose a greater threat to us than the police. We set off after dark on a different route to the Capitol than we had taken the first day and seemed to have gotten further toward that goal. Singing freedom songs had the desired effects I have described but alerted those White people on our route to our presence. Eventually we were stopped by a contingent of Alabama State patrolmen with billy clubs. The patrol was led by Col. Al Lingo, a close associate of Governor Wallace. They wore dark blue uniforms and lighter blue hard hats. What did *they* need the hard hats for? They had the billy clubs. We were stopped in an area near a large highway and in an area where we could sit down in a large group. The patrolmen surrounded our group of several hundred. I kept thinking that this was the same group that killed Jimmie Lee Jackson. One of these patrolmen was a killer and would just as soon kill us as well. It is doubtful that Jackson's killer was in this group, but such were the kind of thoughts that ran through my mind as we sat there waiting to see what might happen next. As had happened yesterday, Forman was in deep conversation with the officer in charge of the patrol. What they discussed I have no idea, but again it went on and on. We passed the time singing and talking in small groups. In my immediate area the conversation among the Alabama State students involved ways of defeating the segregationist system. Not all of the ideas were non-violent. There was the suggestion of putting strychnine in the water supply of White areas and other impractical acts of revenge. I took these to be signs of bravado in the face of being stuck in a non-violent march surrounded by armed White patrolmen.

Suddenly, someone with a transistor radio said that the President was speaking to Congress on civil rights. Sure enough, we could hear the slow Texas drawl of Lyndon Baines Johnson outlining a plan for legislation to support the voting rights of all American citizens regardless of their skin color. He also seemed to endorse the right of Black citizens to protest against the injustices that they faced in America. Suddenly we heard him say, "And we SHALL overcome!" This was an electric moment. Here we were surrounded by the Alabama Highway Patrol, and President Johnson had in effect joined our movement by invoking the anthem of civil rights. It was confusing, exhilarating, and dismaying all at the same time. It was dismaying because his words were not doing the Black people of Alabama a whole lot of good at the moment. There were no Federal troops or FBI protecting our right to protest blocks away from the Alabama state capitol. No cheers went up from our group that night even though this may have been the greatest speech on civil rights ever delivered by an American president before or since. We still had to contend with Forman's negotiations with the Alabama Highway Patrol.

Many within SNCC did not like nor trust President Johnson. The exception was John Lewis who had a close relationship with him. But many within SNCC felt that Johnson had no true understanding of nor connection with black people but was a political opportunist and would do only what he was forced to do on civil rights. For example, SNCC was outraged that Johnson made a fuss over the killing of the White Reverend Reeb in Selma, sending his wife condolences but Johnson did nothing in the face of the killing of Jimmie Lee Jackson who was Black. They also cited the fact that Johnson's legislative record on civil rights was not good when he was in Congress. He voted his White Southern roots.

Johnson's speech was experienced by the White South, however, as a mortal blow. The white mayor of Selma was quoted as saying that he felt as though Johnson had stabbed Dixie in the heart. White southerners never forgave Johnson nor the Democrat Party for that moment. This is the night when the South turned Republican. It took Richard Nixon and his Southern Strategy and Ronald Reagan and his appeals to White grievance to fully implement this change. It was this night when Lyndon Johnson joined the Movement that the South turned Republican.

Nonetheless, I thought something significant and good had happened that night. I just didn't know what its implications were, and I knew we were still in trouble. People were talking about the speech in moderate tones when we got the word that we were to return to our neighborhood. This was starting to form a pattern. We would march, get stopped by the police, Forman would talk, and we would retreat but with the idea of starting again tomorrow.

We started back the way we came, but by this time a large crowd of White men and women lined the path of our retreat on both sides. Our group of about 500 had to walk past a gauntlet of angry White people yelling and screaming at us and close enough to touch us if they wished to. 'N****r this and n****r that', 'white n****r', 'n****r lover' were some of the milder terms hurled at us. We had quite a contingent of White and Back clergy who had come over from Selma where they had gathered at the request of Dr. King and had joined the Montgomery demonstrations. They were subjected to the same taunts. The crowd seemed particularly incensed at the interracial make-up of the march. They seemed to direct their most vicious taunts at the White women and White men in our group. We White men were called 'faggots' and 'queers' while the White women were called 'whores' and 'sluts.' Had there not been a police presence, or if the police had encouraged it, there is no doubt but that this crowd would have done much more than yell and scream. I don't think any of us in the march had ever seen anything like that crowd, and we felt relieved to be back in the High/Jackson neighborhood in one piece.

As psychologists we later had the opportunity to reflect on this experience from a psychological point of view. The anger of the segregationist crowd toward whites who supported blacks in their quest for equal rights was somewhat understandable given the historical, political, and economic circumstances of the South. But what was surprising and not at all self-evident was how quickly, easily, and vociferously sexuality entered into the segregationists' epithets. It seemed that in their world view if White people were involved with Black people, it must be for purposes of sex with Black men. That could be the only reason. The sexualization of race in moments of social change was both powerful and puzzling.

The experience of the angry White crowd dulled our capacity to fully understand the implications of Johnson's speech as well. It seemed very far removed from us. Had Johnson really joined the civil rights movement or was he trying to co-opt us for his own political gain? John Lewis reported later that Dr. King was moved to tears by the speech. Forman said that Johnson had ruined a very good song that night. These were matters for others to ponder. We just wanted to get some sleep before tomorrow came.

Additional Reading

Cash, W.J. (1941). *The Mind of the South.* New York Vintage, 1991.

Goodwin, Doris Kearns (1976). *Lyndon Johnson and the American Dream.* New York: St. Martin's Press.

Smith, Lillian (1944). *Strange Fruit.* San Diego: Harvest, 1992.

Wallace, George C. (1976). *Stand Up for America.* New York: Doubleday.

Photo 8: SNCC workers leading songs at the Jackson Avenue Baptist Church
(Image from the Glen Pearcy Collection, courtesy of the American Folklife Center,
Library of Congress, afc 2012040_041_26)

Photo 9: Willie Ricks leading a non-violent workshop
at the Jackson Avenue Baptist Church
(Image from the Glen Pearcy Collection, courtesy of the American Folklife Center,
Library of Congress, afc 2012040_069_21)

Photo10: John Lewis, SNCC Chairman, addressing marchers outside of the Jackson Avenue Baptist Church (Image courtesy of Rev Norm Hatter)

Photo 11: Marchers stopped by the Alabama State Patrol on a night march. The author is circled. (Image courtesy of Jack Robin Collection, Penn State University Library)

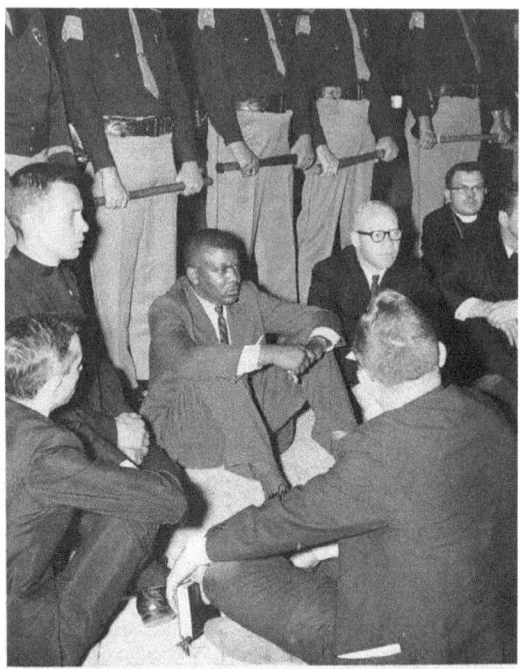

Photo 12: Clergy surrounded by the Alabama State Patrol on the night march
(Image courtesy of Jack Robin Collection, Penn State University Library)

Photo 13: President Johnson addressing Congress on voting rights while marchers
are surrounded by the Alabama State Patrol

Chapter IV

The Third March:
Tuesday, March 16,1965:
The Posse Attacks

We shall not, we shall not be moved.
We shall not, we shall not be moved.
Like a tree that's planted by the waters,
We shall not be moved

The next day brought the best weather yet with warmer temperatures and a hazy sun. We assembled at the empty church building on Jackson Street that had become our headquarters. As we were waiting for the order to move, we were talking with some of the Alabama State students we had met the previous night. There was talk of a mounted posse coming into the neighborhood last night while we were detained by the state troopers. They had gone up on people's porches and beaten them. There was then talk about how to deal with horses if they attacked us today. The idea was to disable the horses with ball bearings. This was more impractical bravado. The idea of being attacked by men on horseback was unsettling. Rory was expecting trouble. He had fashioned a mouth guard out of cellophane and put it between his teeth. The talk about a mounted posse was doubly disconcerting because we had seen the pictures of posse men in Selma on Bloody Sunday just the week before.

Forman writes in his book about Sammy Younge, Jr., the first college student to die in the civil rights struggle, that while we were surrounded by the state patrol the previous night, a mounted sheriff's posse had come into the High and Jackson neighborhood and beaten people and even smashed windows. It was reported by UPI that an ambulance was dispatched but had been prevented from entering the area by the Black residents. It was also reported that the Black residents threw bricks and bottles at the posse. This report, according to Forman, was investigated by SNCC and the part about the detained ambulance found to be wrong; the ambulance was merely parked in the neighborhood. Forman never refuted the part about the posse or the bricks and bottles. We never heard about this, and we lived in the neighborhood at that time. The part about the posse seems plausible and accounts for the rumors of the posse circulating that Tuesday morning. However, I find the story about the bricks and bottles less plausible. It is something that we would have heard about, and it would have brought on a much more massive retaliation from the authorities. I believe that the posse rode through the neighborhood and beat people and destroyed property, but the part about violent retaliation is dubious.

Forman wrote that the ambulance story was part of a disinformation campaign by the SCLC, Reverend James Bevel in particular, to discredit SNCC as leading people to violence and ruining Dr. King's campaign in Alabama. SNCC was indeed challenging Dr. King's leadership, but I do not believe that there was any incitement to violence up to this point.

Our march soon began, but this time we were on still another route to the Capitol that took us past Booker T. Washington High

School. This was a segregated high school that was located south of the High and Jackson neighborhood. We marched through the school singing freedom songs and urging the students to join with us on the march. We emptied the school, and many joined us if only to get a day off from school. We encountered no adults to stop this invitation to truancy. We were in high spirits as we proceeded on to the capitol. Reports on this event say we had about 600 marchers. Forman writes that we had 1,000. There were the Tuskegee and Alabama State students, the high school students, a contingent of clergy—rabbis, priests, ministers, nuns—and the largely white Northern students. The University of Michigan had 50 students, Antioch College had 40 students. Little Juniata College had several marchers, several of whom were later hurt badly. Our Michigan group of six were veterans of the two previous marches and by now much more knowledgeable about what SNCC was trying to accomplish with these demonstrations. Forman and Ricks were leading this march, and other SNCC workers served as marshals to keep everyone on the sidewalks and to lead the singing. We were obeying the traffic lights and attempting not to snarl traffic. Here again we were violating a federal court injunction against marching as well as state and local bans on demonstrations, and we were being careful not to jaywalk! We had gone a fair distance toward the Capitol building when a group of about 100 crossed a street when the light turned red. The larger group stopped and waited for the light to change to green. A group of Montgomery police suddenly appeared at the corner of Decatur and Adams streets, and it seemed that they were going to help the larger group to cross the street. Seemingly out of nowhere a group of men on horses charged into the line of march, beating us with long sticks, ropes, and whips. This we later learned was the Montgomery County Sheriff's Posse. The sheriff's name was Mac Sim Butler, and he was present and on horseback. The posse

59

consisted of 16 men on horseback, 6 uniformed deputies and 10 others recruited for the occasion. One account has the 10 recruits as local ranchers, and another account describes them as riders from a visiting rodeo. In any case, they were vicious. Not content with merely dispersing the marchers, they attacked individuals relentlessly and violently.

Willie Ricks started yelling, "White people to the front! White people to the front!" It was clear what he wanted to do. He wanted to weaponize White skin privilege for the Movement. It was one thing for Black children to be attacked by police dogs and fire hoses in Birmingham in 1963, it was another for White students to be beaten by posse men on horses in 1965. SNCC knew that Rev. Reeb's death was treated differently than Jimmie Lee Jackson's by President Johnson. Spilling some White students' blood might have been part of the trap that George Wallace fell into. I had no problem with this strategy. It was, however, impossible for anyone to re-position in the face of this attack that came by surprise and was over rather quickly. I saw the posse chase a White girl until they cornered her and beat her on the head with a long stick. The crowd of marchers had knocked me down when the posse men attacked from behind forcing the marchers forward and many were trampled. I got up quickly and watched as a posse man stood up in his stirrups to get better leverage to beat marchers who had fallen next to me. The image of this man standing up in his stirrups with utter rage on his face is an image that has stuck with me to this day. With so many reporters and cameramen covering this march, news quickly spread of the violence and the casualties.

It was reported that 15 marchers were seriously injured with 8 being taken to the hospital by ambulance. Among those injured was Fran Lipton, a White undergrad from the University of Michigan who was stepped on by a horse. There was a rumor that an Asian-

American student had received a fractured skull. The student turned out to be Steven K. Kuromiya from the University of Pennsylvania. He was indeed clubbed and then trampled by a horse. He was taken by ambulance to a hospital. The march was halted, and the marchers dispersed. Rory and Jim had taken off trying to avoid the posse. Forman and Ricks were nowhere to be seen. Our Michigan group met back up and tried to decide what to do next. As we were talking, a group of Montgomery Police on motorcycles tried to run us over. They came up on the sidewalk where we were standing and aimed right at us. None of us had been hurt, and it was not so difficult to dodge out of the way. They made a couple of passes at us and then roared away. We were shaken up by all of this and a little unsure of exactly where we were. We felt exposed and at the mercy of forces whose sole aim seemed to be to do us great bodily harm. There were only a few stragglers from the march on the sidewalk who seemed disoriented as well.

It is hard to describe the psychological impact this attack had on me. What I was feeling was not fear. It was more like being separated from my surround, from my sense of community. I felt that if I had been injured the community would not help. A White hospital would not treat me, and a Black hospital might not be able to as had just happened to Rev. Reeb. The police and the sheriff were trying to hurt us. The Federal government did not seem interested enough to step in. We were alone with few allies. At the moment our leadership was missing in action. Beyond this I felt that my very identity had been threatened. White skin privilege either did not operate in a situation like this, or it had been stripped away. I had been dehumanized by the posse, treated like a thing to be abused and tossed aside. For what? For standing up for the right to redress grievances against an unjust system and the right to vote? This is what Black people had faced every single day in America, and we just got a small taste of it—the dehumanization, the threat of violence, and the disdain.

A man was suddenly yelling from a pay phone on the street that someone was calling from Detroit asking to talk to someone from Michigan. Being from Detroit I went over to the pay phone to take the call. The caller identified himself as Avern Cohn, a lawyer from Detroit. He had just heard on television that a group of students including those from the University of Michigan had just been attacked and wondered what had happened. I later learned that Mr. Cohn was a partner in one of the most prestigious law firms in Detroit, Honigman, Miller, Schwartz, and Cohn. He was active in Democratic Party politics and was eventually appointed a Federal judge by President Jimmy Carter. I filled him in as best I could about what had just happened. He said that he was a University of Michigan grad and asked me what he could do to help? I blurted out that he should urge the President to send Federal troops to protect civil rights workers because the local police were out to hurt us as had just happened. This was something that SNCC had very much wanted in their work in community development in Alabama, Mississippi, and Georgia. He said that he would work on it in a very earnest and heartfelt tone. I hung up a little stunned that someone had reached out to us on a street corner in Montgomery, Alabama so quickly. How do you call a pay phone on a street corner? If SNCC's strategy was to keep the pressure on and to sucker George Wallace into further violence that could be witnessed around the country and that violence was aimed not only at Black people but at young White people as well, then the strategy worked.

I went back to our small group to tell them about the phone call. We were still wondering if we were headed in the right direction when a blue Buick sedan came down the otherwise deserted street and stopped in front us. I was closest to the curb. The rear window rolled down and there was Dr. Martin Luther King, Jr. "How y'all doin'?" he said. "What happened?" I was the closest to him. "We're not doing very well, Dr. King." I filled him in on what had happened. We knew that he was not in favor of the marches in Montgomery, that he favored waiting for Judge Johnson's ruling. He was on his way to the Federal courthouse when he apparently heard of the posse's attack.

Rory, prone to the most radical pole of an issue, began a silent protest against Dr. King by lying down in front of his car. Dr. King did not seem to notice but if he did, he must have thought that SNCC had attracted some pretty crazy White kids.

Dr. King seemed genuinely interested in where we were from and what we were doing in Montgomery. By this time a small group had assembled and wanted to talk to Dr. King. I noticed the other occupants of Dr. King's car. In the back seat was a Black man I did not recognize and an attractive woman wearing a black dress. In the front seat was a Black man who was the driver and an older White man. All the men were dressed in dark suits and ties.

Seeing the attractive woman immediately reminded me of a talk that Malcolm X gave at Harvard in 1962. Malcolm said that he had hard evidence that a civil rights leader who was Baptist preacher was unfaithful to his wife. Malcolm never said what that evidence was nor how he had obtained it. It was common knowledge in the civil rights movement that Dr. King had a roving eye. I assumed, perhaps wrongly, that this woman in the back seat was sleeping with Dr. King. I had no evidence for this, it was just a random thought that I kept to myself.

I also thought that the woman was possibly White. Reverend Ralph Abernathy later wrote an autobiography in which he detailed King's struggle with adultery. Abernathy was criticized for this breach of personal privacy.

I learned much later that Dr. King sometimes traveled with a very light-skinned woman from Atlanta who was also a friend of Mrs. Coretta Scott King. I believe now that this woman I saw in Montgomery with Dr. King was Xernona Clayton. Mrs. Clayton had recently joined SCLC in 1965 and had moved to Atlanta. She later became the first Black person in the South to have her own television show, and she was responsible for leading the effort to desegregate hospital facilities in Atlanta.

The White man from the front seat got out of the car and introduced himself to me. He said he was Harry Boyte. I was stunned again. I knew who Harry Boyte was! He had lived in Monroe, North Carolina and had been a supporter of Robert Williams in the late 50's, and it was rumored that he had helped Williams escape to Canada in the aftermath of the 1961 riot and charges of kidnapping. The Boyte family must have had deep roots in Monroe because the street that Williams lived on was named Boyte Street. I later learned that Boyte was the first White employee of SCLC and served as advisor to Dr. King. So as Dr. King talked to the group of marchers that had assembled, I talked to Harry Boyte about the coincidence of my having been in Monroe, and we chatted about Williams and the trumped-up charges against him.

I got the distinct impression from talking with Dr. King and Harry Boyte that day that they believed that our march had either turned violent or was about to turn violent in the aftermath of the posse's attack. Dr. King's goal in talking to us seemed to be to calm our feelings and restore the approach of non-violence. This was puzzling to me at the time because our preparation for these marches and this march itself were non-violent. The attack of the posse was unprovoked and seemed to be planned. However, John Lewis who had been staying with Dr. King at the Ben Moore Hotel, later wrote in his autobiography that the posse attacked us in retaliation for the marchers' throwing bricks and bottles at them. This echoes the story of the Black crowd throwing bricks and bottles at the posse men the night before when we were surrounded by the Alabama State Highway Patrol. It is possible that Lewis, who was not at the march on Tuesday, conflated these two events and believed that the marchers had broken the non-violent code. It is also possible that both stories as well as the story about the ambulance being stopped, was disinformation promoted by law enforcement and believed by SCLC.

The idea that this march turned violent, and that the posse retaliated is false and illogical on several counts. First, I was there and while I was not in a position to see the entire line of march, and notwithstanding the bravado about thwarting horses with ball bearings, I would have seen or heard later about such a momentous thing as marchers throwing bricks and bottles at the posse in broad daylight. The attack of the posse was a complete surprise to us. They came out of nowhere and the attack seemed to be for no reason. In retrospect, the posse used the opportunity of the red light separating the two parts of the march, to attack. Even discounting my account as an eyewitness, the charge of violence on the part of the marchers seems ridiculous for other reasons. In the climate of tension and hatred that existed at the time on the part of the segregationists, any violent resistance on the part of civil rights demonstrators would have been met with lethal force. Two civil rights marchers had recently been killed, and it seems unthinkable that violent resistance would not have resulted in many more casualties. The posse was simply breaking up the demonstration with as much force as they could get away with. The other factor that makes it implausible that the marchers were violent is that this march was covered by a very large contingent of news reporters and photographers from news outlets all over the country.

They were just waiting for violence as that is what made the news. If the marchers had started the violence this would have been seen and reported by this very large group of reporters and photographers. The bricks and bottles were perhaps conflated with the anecdotal reports of the night before. The best account of the posse's attack I have read came from the *Harvard Crimson* and the student reporter, Peter Cummings. He had a full and detailed account of the posse's attack. There was no mention of any violence, instigating or retaliatory, on the part of the marchers.

John Lewis wrote that this was a violent demonstration on the part of the marchers and Dr. King and SCLC apparently believed in this scenario as well. Lewis wrote in his autobiography:

When the police began pushing in and physically shoving the students aside, some of the students responded by throwing rocks, bricks, and bottles. This brought the posse men forward, swinging clubs and whips. When the students ran, the posse men chased them on horseback, actually riding up onto porches of private homes (Lewis, 1998, pp. 338–339).

The last part is accurate, but this sequence is not accurate and there was no provocative or retaliatory attack on the police. Lewis was not there and where he got this information is not clear. However, the account of marcher violence is what brought Dr. King into the streets shortly after the posse and the motorcycle police had tried to run over us. But violence on our part never happened. How are we to explain this?

The Subversive Unit of the Alabama Highway Patrol, the "Red Squad" that many states had at that time, took several photographs of this march. A series of these photos are in the Jack Rabin Collection

66

at the Penn State University Library. One of these photos seems out of place and not quite understandable. It depicts a crumbling brick wall with several loose bricks. When I saw this photo among the others showing the demonstrators and the posse, I wondered if the Subversive Unit was trying to document that these were examples of bricks used by the demonstrators to attack the posse. If needed later, this could be used as evidence later that the posse acted in self-defense.

It seems to me more plausible that the story of marcher violence was disinformation circulated by law enforcement to justify the unprovoked attack on the marchers. This disinformation was picked up by SCLC and believed because of the increasing tension between SNCC and SCLC. SCLC was afraid that Forman's militancy was going to derail Dr. King's plan for the Alabama voting rights movement. I have tried to delineate the differences between SNCC and SCLC and a rift between these organizations was becoming deeper. They were in competition for the allegiance of the Black people of Alabama, particularly the students.

I thought at the time that this attack by the posse was the segregationist answer to President Johnson's 'We shall overcome' declaration. The mayor of Selma, Joe Smitherman, characterized Johnson's speech as "a dagger to the heart of Dixie." Whether the order for the posse to charge came directly from Governor Wallace or whether it came from the Sheriff Mac Sim Butler of Montgomery County or from spontaneous combustion, the message was clear— segregation was not going to fall without drawing blood.

Rory had abandoned his sit-in in front of Dr. King's car. Dr. King told us again to come to a meeting that night at the Beulah Baptist Church where there would be a "big announcement." As he was pulling away from the curb, I shook Dr. King's hand to Rory's disapproval, I am sure. Forman in his account of that day writes that he met with Dr.

King that afternoon to discuss the issue of the ministers in Montgomery and their refusal to allow SNCC to use church buildings. Dr. King had told us where the meeting was to be held, Beulah Baptist Church, so he had already worked out something before he met with Forman that afternoon. It was more of the politics between King, Forman, and the local ministers who supported King. It is to be remembered that both King and Ralph Abernathy had begun their careers as civil rights activists as pastors of Montgomery churches.

The article by Peter Cummings and documented in photos made by Glenn Pearcy, a reporter/photographer for the *Harvard Crimson,* indicates that many marchers returned to the Jackson Street Baptist Church where they were addressed on the street outside by Forman and Rev. Bevel. Bevel's presence is most interesting, given his belief that the marches were turning violent and hurting Dr. King's program. Pearcy's photos also indicate that a large contingent of Montgomery Police on motorcycles were also present at this Jackson Street gathering. They must have followed the marchers back after trying to run us down on the sidewalk earlier.

Unfortunately, our small Michigan group was not present on Jackson Street to hear what Forman and Bevel had to say. We were rather shaken by the attack and decided to go back to where we were staying and re-group mentally for the meeting that evening. However, the *Crimson* reporter includes some direct quotes from Bevel who seemed to be arguing with some students who were urging retaliatory violence against the police. By the end of the meeting Bevel and Forman had managed to calm the crowd who were very angry. Forman, himself, was very angry as became evident later that evening.

We had made our way back to the High and Jackson neighborhood, got a quick bite of dinner, and headed over to the Beulah Baptist

Church. This church must have been chosen as a neutral site as neither King nor Abernathy had pastored this particular church.

By the time we got there, the church was filled. There were TV and film cameras and as many reporters as citizens. I could not get a place inside, so I stood on a small porch just outside a side door. The sound system was very good, and I heard every word. Standing next to me was another surprise in the form of a man named Jim Laue. Jim had been a graduate student in social psychology at Harvard and was the teaching assistant in Professor Tom Pettigrew's course on the social psychology of the civil rights movement when I took it. After getting his Ph.D., Jim had joined the Civil Rights Division of the Justice Department. He was serving as an "observer" for the Justice Department and was monitoring the events in Montgomery as well as Selma. I gave him an earful of what had happened that day and asked him why there were no marshals or troops to protect the rights of citizens. He was sympathetic but non-committal.

The meeting started with prayers and the singing of freedom songs. Forman gave a speech that is remembered as his most important one. He said:

There's only one man in the country that can stop George Wallace and those posses. We can present thousands of bodies in the streets if we want to and and we can do all the soul searching and the moral commitment around the world. But these problems will not be solved until the man in that shaggedy (sic) old place called the White House begins to shake and gets on the phone and says, "Now listen, George, we're comin' down there and throw you in jail if you don't stop that mess." (applause) That's how this is going to get solved. It's not just the sheriff of this county or the mayor or George Wallace. This problem goes to the very bottom of the United States. And, you know, I said it today and I will say it again. If we can't sit at the table [of democracy] let's knock the f***ing legs off! (softly) Excuse me (Quoted in Lewis, 1996, p. 340).

There was no applause, a little rustling, and some murmuring. I looked at Jim Laue, and he looked at me. I whispered to him, "Did he say that in church?" Jim just rolled his eyes. Everyone seemed shocked. This line became the one that James Forman is most remembered for. Forman later explained his use of profanity as coming from his outrage at the attack of the posse that afternoon. However, this demonstration marked the last non-violent march in which Forman would ever participate, and this speech marked a turning point in militancy for Forman and for SNCC as well.

Rev. Ralph Abernathy was next, and he introduced Dr. King. Abernathy must have been a little shaken up by Forman's profanity as well. He introduced King as the "Pharaoh of the 20th Century" instead of its "Moses." Again, I looked at Jim and he looked at me. "Did I hear what I thought I heard?" I asked him. He nodded affirmatively and whispered to me that in the '50s Abernathy and King had been competitors for the leadership of the Montgomery Improvement Association prior to the bus boycott. Apparently, they were competitors still. It did not take a pair of psychologists to realize that this was a Freudian slip of major proportions. Nobody took notice, Dr. King thanked Rev. Abernathy for the introduction, and proceeded to give his speech. He never addressed Forman's remarks directly but expressed the need for non-violence directed in an appropriate way. In the middle of his speech, he announced that Judge Frank Johnson had lifted his injunction against marches, and that the Selma to Montgomery march would take place. This was greeted with loud applause. Dr. King also announced then that there would be a march to the county courthouse the next day to protest the violence of the sheriff's posse, and that plans for the Selma to Montgomery march would commence immediately. This was met with more loud applause. There had been an apparent victory.

In the tug of war between SNCC and SCLC, it appeared that SCLC had retaken the leadership of the Movement in Alabama and that it was Dr. King, not SNCC, who had delivered the victory. Dr. King had tried to demonstrate that his approach, restraint and working with the reasonable elements of the power structure, would bring results. By contrast, he implied that SNCC would bring violence, chaos, and reprisal.

I left the church that night confused and with all the events of the day swirling around in my head. I found Forman's remarks thrilling and certainly reflecting a portion of my feelings of frustration at the amount of sacrifice and patience required to effect change. But I felt that the judge's ruling was important, and that something good had come out of this tumultuous day.

Additional Reading

Ralph David Abernathy (1989). *And the Walls Came Tumbling Down: An Autobiography.* New York: Harper and Row

James Forman (1968). *Sammy Younge, Jr.: The First Black College Student to Die in the Black Liberation Movement.* New York: Grove Press.

John Lewis (1998). *Walking with the Wind: A Memoir of the Movement.* New York: Simon and Schuster.

Photo 14: Willie Ricks leading singing while march is stopped by the Montgomery Police. The author is circled. (Image from the Glen Pearcy Collection, courtesy of the American Folklife Center, Library of Congress, afc 2012040_045_14)

Photo 15: The march to the state capitol resumes. The author is circled. (Image from the Glen Pearcy Collection, courtesy of the American Folklife Center, Library of Congress, afc 2012040_044_30)

Photo 16: The posse attacks marchers on horseback. The author is circled.

Photo 17: A marcher is attacked by posse men.
(Image from the Glen Pearcy Collection, courtesy of the American Folklife Center,
Library of Congress, afc 2012040_045_37)

Photo 18: Injured marcher
(Image from the Glen Pearcy Collection, courtesy of the American Folklife Center,
Library of Congress, afc 2012040_048_02)

Photo 19: Injured marcher
(Image from the Glen Pearcy Collection, courtesy of the American Folklife Center,
Library of Congress, afc 2012040_046_43)

Photo 20: Injured marcher
(Image from the Glen Pearcy Collection, courtesy of the American Folklife Center,
Library of Congress, afc 2012040_046_41)

Photo 21: James Forman and Rev. James Bevel of SCLC try to calm the angry Marchers. (Image from the Glen Pearcy Collection, courtesy of the American Folklife Center, Library of Congress, afc 2012040_047_01)

Photo 22: Dr. Martin Luther King, Jr. of SCLC announces that Judge Johnson Approved the Selma to Montgomery march. (Image from the Glen Pearcy Collection, courtesy of the American Folklife Center, Library of Congress, afc 2012040_051_04)

Photo 23: James Forman denounces the posse attack. (Image from the Glen Pearcy Collection, courtesy of the American Folklife Center, Library of Congress, afc 2012040_050_03)

Chapter V

The Fourth March: Wednesday, March 17, 1965: To the Sheriff

We shall overcome.
We shall overcome.
We shall overcome, someday.

The next morning, we assembled for the announced march to the county sheriff's office. The weather was decidedly overcast, and it had begun to rain. Leading the march were John Lewis, Martin Luther King, Jr., James Foreman, Ralph Abernathy, and several black ministers both local and from out of state. Other members of the front rows of Marchers included local Montgomery leaders who had been involved in the Montgomery Bus Boycott of ten years earlier. The men, except for Forman, wore their characteristic dark suits and ties. Forman was wearing a dark suit coat and dark tie over his bib overalls. The front line of march began with their arms locked together. Whatever the tensions and differences of the past, these were temporarily forgotten as the march proceeded in the rain. There was an American Flag and a United Nations flag, a feature I had never seen before. There must have been 1,000 people in this march as many of SCLC supporters had come over from Selma to swell the ranks. These included Andrew Young and the Rev. C.T Vivian. Vivian was 6'5" or 6'6" and always stood out in a crowd!

We had heard rumors that members of the Nation of Islam from Birmingham were protecting the line of march that day. I am skeptical about this as it seems unlikely that the NOI would want anything to do with the civil rights movement particularly so soon after the assassination of Malcolm X. But it gave us something to talk about as we waited three hours in the rain as the leaders talked to the Sheriff Butler and other officials in the dry county building. It was reported that the sheriff apologized for the excessive use of violence by the posse. We certainly never heard this at the time, and no one conveyed this to the crowd of marchers.

The sheriff is also reported to have said that the posse's charge was due to a "miscommunication." When the two groups split up when the stop light turned red, the Sheriff said that he ordered the posse to get the first group back with the second group. The posse misunderstood and attacked. The sheriff's account has found its way into historical accounts. It seems very implausible. In his account, Forman notes that a group of Montgomery police suddenly showed up at the corner where the larger group of marchers had stopped for the light and prevented them from moving. Forman's account is incomplete because he believed that the posse had only attacked the small group he was leading. Photographs clearly show that the posse also attacked the rear of the large group of marchers herding them forward and then attacking those who ran. This is how I was knocked down. So, from my experience and the photographic evidence this was a coordinated attack by the posse with help from the Montgomery Police. The sheriff did not, however, claim that the posse acted in self-defense with the marchers' throwing bricks and bottles, as John Lewis reported in his autobiography. At the conclusion of the meeting Dr. King emerged and addressed the crowd, announcing to this group that the march from Selma to Montgomery was to take place in a matter of days. This was greeted with loud applause.

This march, however, was anti-climactic compared to the events of the day before. As I mentioned we never heard that the Sheriff apologized, and even if we did it would not have made much difference. We felt vaguely that we had accomplished something and the right to march was seen as a victory. The President of the United States had pledged support for voting rights legislation and had put the weight of his office behind the movement for civil rights. However, from where we were located geographically and psychologically, we believed that segregation was far from beaten.

When we returned to the place we were staying, hoping for some warm food and warm clothes, the young man informed us that we would have to leave. His White landlord and employer had found out that he was boarding civil rights people. He was threatened with eviction and the loss of his job. We felt very badly for him and guilty that his hospitality had put his family in danger.

We held a quick meeting. While we had no definite date for going back to Ann Arbor, it seemed to be the consensus that we should leave tomorrow and use the last march as our last contribution to SNCC in Montgomery. We probably could have found another place to stay and the prospect of the Selma to Montgomery march was very tempting. We were, however, psychologically beaten up and weary. We started getting our stuff gathered up and said goodbye to the young man, his wife, and baby and thanked them for everything they had done for us. We hoped that there would not be retaliation against them for housing and feeding us.

SNCC arranged for us to stay in another house nearby. A man moved his family to a relative's house for the night. We stayed in the master bedroom. The stress of the week culminated in a flash of temper as we tried to decide who was going to sleep in the bed and who would sleep on the floor. We had all gotten along very well through the week but for some reason nerves were on edge that night.

There were rumors of White reprisals against those local people who were helping SNCC and the out-of-town marchers. The man in whose house we were staying had a rifle and shotgun and assured us that no harm was going to come to us. He stayed up all night on his front porch with his shotgun on his lap and his rifle propped next to him. We never asked him for this show of courage, but we were grateful for it. It also fit more the model of Robert Williams' brand of armed self-defense than non-violence, but no one in our group thought it amiss. The man was defending his home as well as us!

Until recently the role of armed self-defense in the Civil Rights Movement has not been well known. Two recent books on this subject, one by Charles Cobb of SNCC and another by Professor Akinyele Umoja of Georgia State, describe the role of armed resistance especially in Mississippi. The actions of the man who stayed up all night protecting us with his rifle and shotgun was thus not unusual. It was necessary under the circumstances even if our commitment in the marches was non-violent. Professor Umoja makes a distinction in his discussion of armed resistance in Mississippi between armed self-defense, retaliatory violence, spontaneous rebellion, and various forms of offensive resistance like guerilla warfare, armed enforcement, and armed struggle to gain state power. Umoja claims that all these forms of armed resistance were present in the Mississippi freedom movement into the 1970's. We experienced only armed self-defense which I know we were all thankful for.

Shotgun in hand, he woke us up before dawn. I oversaw our departure, and I wanted to get an early start out of Montgomery under the cover of some darkness so as not to call too much attention to ourselves. The group had trouble getting up that morning and dawn broke before we actually got going.

Additional Reading

Charles E. Cobb, Jr. (2014). *This Nonviolent Stuff'll Get You Killed: How Guns Made the Civil Rights Movement Possible.* New York: Basic Books.

Akinyele Omowale Umoja (2013). *We Will Shoot Back: Armed Resistance in the Mississippi Freedom Movement.* New York: New York University Press.

Photo 24: The march to the Sheriff's Office begins in solidarity. (Image from the Glen Pearcy Collection, courtesy of the American Folklife Center, Library of Congress, afc 2012040_054_19)

Photo 25: The clergy prepares for the march reading SNCC's newspaper. (Image from the Glen Pearcy Collection, courtesy of the American Folklife Center, Library of Congress, afc 2012040_053_16)

Photo 26: Dr King announces the results of the meeting with the Sheriff. (Image from the Glen Pearcy Collection, courtesy of the American Folklife Center, Library of Congress, afc 2012040_056_03)

Photo 27: Marchers listen to Dr. King and other speakers. (Image from the Glen Pearcy Collection, courtesy of the American Folklife Center, Library of Congress, afc 2012040_056_18)

Chapter VI

March 19, 1965: Returning Home

I woke up this mornin'
with my mind
Stayed on freedom.
Woke up this mornin' with my mind on freedom
Stayed on freedom.
Woke up this mornin' with my mind
Stayed on freedom
Hallelu, hallelu, hallelujah.

I'm walkin' and talking with my mind
Stayed on freedom.
I'm walkin' and talkin' with my mind
Stayed on freedom
I'm walkin' and talkin' with my mind
Stayed on freedom.
Hallelu, hallelu, hallelujah.

Before we left Montgomery, I told the group that I was going to travel right at the speed limit so as not to draw the attention of law enforcement. Dawn was just about breaking when we said our good-byes to the man who had stayed up all night protecting us. I was mindful of the fact that the three civil rights workers in Mississippi were stopped by the Neshoba County Sheriff and jailed before being handed over to the Ku Klux Klan to be killed. I also asked the passengers to stay awake and be alert for cars passing us on the left and any signs that someone could shoot at us out of the car windows. Everyone agreed to this plan. We took state highway 80 out of Montgomery and had agreed to go home through Atlanta where we could stop at SNCC headquarters on Raymond Street. After the rain of yesterday, the morning was cloudless and sunny. As soon as we hit the highway, all the passengers fell asleep. Not only did they fall asleep, but they all hunched down a little below the window line. I was mad because they were leaving me to both drive and watch out for snipers, but I didn't have heart to wake them up.

Highway 80 was four lanes wide and at this early hour traffic was light. Several cars passed me on the left and I kept a wary eye out for signs of guns. I would hunch down a little whenever a car passed me. I may have been unduly cautious or even a bit paranoid. However, bad things had happened in Alabama, and I did not want to become a casualty or a martyr. As the saying goes, just because you're paranoid doesn't mean somebody's not out to get you! It was a tense ride for me as several more cars passed me, and my passengers slept through Alabama. Finally, we hit the Georgia state line. Welcome to the Peach State!

As if by magic or some previously arranged signal everyone woke up! All the pent-up stress of the week had been released. Everyone was animated and in high spirits, joking and laughing. All the tensions of the night before had vanished as well. This made me even madder, and I reminded everyone that the state of Georgia was still segregated and that we were still at risk. They ignored me, but I was relieved, too. Georgia was not Alabama or Mississippi after all.

We proceeded into Atlanta and stopped at the SNCC office. We were hoping to meet Julian Bond, but he was not there that day and all of the other field secretaries were still in Alabama and other hot spots. The only person in the office that day was Dorothy "Dottie" Miller Zellner. I had known Dottie when I was helping to raise money for SNCC in Boston. She sent several SNCC workers from Mississippi up to Boston for R and R, and it was my job to show them a good time. I had somehow gained the reputation for expertise in the Boston area night life. Dottie was married to Bob Zellner, the first White SNCC field secretary. She had started with CORE and was arrested in Miami and later in SNCC demonstrations in Danville, Virginia known as "Bloody Danville." Forman recruited her for SNCC, and she worked with Julian Bond on SNCC's newspaper, *The Student Voice*. She became the public relations coordinator for SNCC in all respects and ran the many Friends of SNCC efforts in the North. I was happy to meet her in person, and she was eager to hear news about Montgomery. She loaded us up with newspapers and other materials to take back to Ann Arbor for distribution. We thanked her, packed up, and headed home.

Unbeknownst to us, a counter march was taking place in Montgomery that day. Glen Pearcy, a student photographer for the *Harvard Crimson*, documented this march by white citizens protesting President Johnson, Martin Luther King, Jr., and civil rights for Black people in general. The march seems to have taken place on Dexter Avenue to the capitol building. The signs the White marchers carried the unmistakable message of a White backlash:

"Fire N****r Workers," "N****r go Home," States Rights Forever," "Larger White Marches Coming," "Hire Whites Only," "Johnson's a Communist Dictator, "Resist Civil Rights

Bill," "Who Needs N****rs," "Where are White Civil Rights,"
"Bnai Brith is anti-Christian," Impeach N****r Lover Johnson,"
"LBJ and MLK are Going to Ruin the USA."

The significance of this march lies in the narrative of White grievance
that is still relevant today. The march was supposed to be an answer
to Judge Johnson's ruling in favor of civil rights marches as lawful
and to President Johnson's endorsement of the aims of the civil
rights movement especially in the area of voting rights. The logic
of the sign, "Where are White Civil Rights," is the grievance that
granting ordinary civil rights to Blacks constitutes taking away rights
from Whites. This zero-sum logic is still operative today particularly
in affirmative action where efforts to redress past wrongs to Blacks
is conceived as depriving Whites of their rights. The sign depicting
"Bnai Brith is anti-Christian" is hard to understand in the context of
1965 other than the idea that somehow Jews are behind the Blacks'
quest for civil rights and thus the civil rights movement was against
White Christians. The fact that B'nai B'rith was on the minds of
White people in Montgomery was very surprising to me. While B'nai
B'rith, a Jewish social service organization, supports human rights and
works against anti-Semitism, it was not a civil rights organization. The
marcher might have meant to disparage the Anti-Defamation League
which was at one time a part of B'nai B'rith but became a separate
organization in 1915 after the lynching of a Jewish man, Leo Frank,
in Atlanta. With the current rise of anti-Semitism in the United States,
it is interesting to note this instance of an anti-Semitic element in this
White counter-protest in 1965. The overall message of this counter-
protest was that Black progress of any kind means a loss for White
people—economic, political, and identity-wise.

We were spared the spectacle of this White grievance and returned to Ann Arbor the next day and tried to get our lives back to normal. I had missed a statistics exam, and the professor was not happy with my reasons for missing it. It was only through the intercession of Professor Mann that I was allowed to take a make-up exam. Rory, Jim, and I gave a lecture to the 1200 students in Psychology 101 about our experiences and we gave an interview to WUOM, the campus radio station. On March 21, after we had returned, Dr. King led 3200 marchers out of Selma, across the Edmund Pettus Bridge toward Montgomery, and they reached the state capitol on March 25. I watched some of the march on television and felt a pang of regret that we had not stayed for this event. We knew that the SNCC leaders were conflicted about this march, and it was clear that Dr. King had seized control of the movement in Alabama and was being given credit for "the victory."

Forman did not participate in the march. In fact, after we left Forman continued to lead demonstrations in Montgomery for several days that resulted in many arrests. He seemed to be trying to further radicalize the Tuskegee and Alabama State students and to give them an alternative to Dr. King's leadership. Those arrested were sent not to the Montgomery city jail but to the notorious Kilby State Prison that housed the electric chair dubbed "Yellow Mama." This prison was in such bad shape that it was closed in 1969. Those SNCC protesters arrested missed the opening days of the Selma to Montgomery march. If we had stayed, there was a good chance that we would have participated in these demonstrations and would have ended up in Kilby also. Forman writes in his autobiography that the march during which we were attacked by the posse was his last large-scale civil rights march.

Stokely Carmichael, soon to replace John Lewis as Chairman of SNCC, had been working in Lowndes County, Alabama developing a grass roots political movement outside of the Democratic or Republican parties. Carmichael did not take part in Forman's Montgomery demonstrations but continued to work in Lowndes. When the march came through Lowndes County, however, he joined Dr. King briefly on the march. Carmichael was to play a pivotal role in shifting the focus of SNCC from a non-violent, inter-racial civil rights organization to a more radical group with a black nationalist revolutionary agenda.

The Selma marchers arrived in Montgomery on March 25 and heard speeches by Dr. King, Rev. Abernathy, Rev. Fred Shuttlesworth from Birmingham, Rosa Parks, Ralph Bunche, Whitney Young of the Urban League, and others. At the conclusion of the march activists were shuttled to airports, train stations, and bus stations to return home. One of the drivers was Mrs. Viola Liuzzo, a 39-year-old White housewife from Detroit who had come to Selma to help with the voter registration drive after Bloody Sunday. On that day she was returning from the Montgomery airport with a Black 19-year-old local resident named Leroy Moton along State Highway 80 outside of Montgomery. Four Ku Klux Klansmen pulled up alongside Liuzzo's 1963 Oldsmobile, and she was shot twice in the head. Moton, who was not hit, was covered in blood and pretended to be dead when the Klansmen checked the car. Moton eventually flagged down a car driven by another civil rights worker and escaped.

This was exactly the scenario that I was concerned about when we left Montgomery a few days earlier on Highway 80. I was not so paranoid after all!

There were some complicating factors that made this tragic death even worse.

Four men were arrested for the murder within 24 hours because one of the four men in the car was an FBI paid informant, Gary Rowe. President Johnson announced the arrests on national television but did not mention the FBI connection. Three men were indicted in state court for Liuzzo's murder, and the FBI informant was a witness even though he may have himself fired into the car.

The three men were easily acquitted with the defense attorney characterizing the victim as a "white n****r." They were given a celebratory parade. The three were then tried on federal charges with conspiracy to intimidate African-Americans under the 1871 Ku Klux Klan Act. They were found guilty and sentenced to ten years in Federal prison. Gary Rowe went into the witness protection program because of threats on his life.

Almost immediately after the murder of Mrs. Liuzzo, the FBI began a secret disinformation campaign to impugn her character. The FBI started rumors that she was a drug addict, had had sex with Moton, and that her husband, Anthony, a Teamsters union official, was part of organized crime in Detroit. Her autopsy eventually showed no trace of drugs or alcohol and that she had not had sex recently. There was no evidence ever uncovered that Anthony Liuzzo had any ties to organized crime. It was smear campaign pure and simple. The FBI's motive seems to have been an attempt to distract attention away from the fact that a paid FBI informant failed to stop the murder and may have even participated by firing his gun into the car. Instead, the FBI tried to smear the victim. It seems to be another shameful chapter in the history of the FBI's relationship to the civil rights movement.

A couple of days after we returned to Ann Arbor on March 24 and into March 25, we took part in the first "teach-in" against the war in Viet Nam. It was not the largest teach-in, but it was the first. It was the idea of University of Michigan anthropology professor Marshall

Sahlins, and he was joined by a number of other professors including Richard Mann, the social psychologist Bill Gamson, the historian Charles Tilley and others. SDS organized the students and over 3500 attended speeches, workshops, and rallies that lasted over-night and into the morning. The anti-war movement captured the attention of a great many students in the north, east, and west and siphoned off some of the energy for civil rights efforts in the South.

The major players in the Selma-Montgomery marches took varied paths. Lyndon Johnson made good on his pledge to see voting rights legislation through the Congress. In the summer, the Voting Rights Act of 1965 was passed with bi-partisan support. Johnson had already gotten the 1964 Civil Rights Act passed which outlawed discrimination in public accommodations and the Civil Rights Act of 1968 prohibited discrimination in housing. These proved to be the most significant accomplishments of the Civil Rights Movement and they would not have happened without Lyndon Johnson.

In addition, Johnson developed what he termed the Great Society and proposed measures that strengthened health care (Medicare and Medicaid), early education (Head Start), job training, economic development in the cities, environmental protection, consumer rights, urban transportation initiatives, and other legislation aimed at improving the condition of poor people in America. This agenda was largely overshadowed by the escalation of the war in Vietnam and the protests against it. This war and the divisiveness in the country that followed from it cost Johnson his presidency as well as his legacy of ending segregation and battling poverty. He was forced not to seek re-election in 1968. The assassination of Robert Kennedy and the debacle of the 1968 Democratic Party Convention in Chicago left a weakened Democratic Party and resulted in the election of Republican Richard M. Nixon. In four short years the Democrats had seen a landslide victory give way to an ignominious defeat. How did this happen? I shall have more to say about this in my final chapter, but I believe it had to do, at least in part, with some failures of the Civil Rights Movement itself.

George Wallace was also politically prominent after the marches in Selma and Montgomery. The reader should recall that Wallace forced Lyndon Johnson to federalize the Alabama National Guard, so that Wallace could claim that the Federal government was protecting the civil rights marchers, not the state of Alabama. This became part of Wallace's narrative that the Federal government was imposing integration on states that had the right to support segregation. Wallace decided to run for president and in 1968 got more votes than any other third-party candidate in the 20th century. He carried Arkansas, Louisiana, Mississippi, Alabama, and Georgia and did well in white working-class areas in the North. These same voters were later to be called Reagan Democrats!

Wallace brought his 1968 campaign to Ann Arbor, and we were ready for him. We set up a very large and vocal protest outside of Hill Auditorium where he gave his speech. We were restrained by barricades set up by the student-friendly Ann Arbor police. While Wallace was railing against hippies and pointy-headed professors we were railing against him. At one point in the evening, his security detail from Alabama came out of the auditorium to taunt us. We let them have it with every profanity we could think of. They seemed slightly amused but retreated.

Apparently, inside the auditorium Wallace did not fare too well either. The beating of University of Michigan students in Montgomery was not forgotten and not forgiven. He was constantly interrupted and booed by the raucous crowd of students. This reaction only fed into the Wallace narrative, and the shouts of civil rights-minded students only cemented Wallace's bond with those Americans who resisted racial and economic change. We loved shouting at him, and he welcomed this so he could show that he was standing up against the civil rights-loving hippies and communists. The success of the Wallace campaign particularly in the North was dismaying and disquieting as the late sixties were beginning to see the backlash from the civil rights demonstrations in the South and the urban insurrections (riots) in the North and West. The Republicans were beginning to see a "Southern strategy" by which they could use the White Southern vote to garner support for the Republican Party. The Wallace campaign for president ended when he was shot at a rally.

James Forman said that he would never take part in another large-scale non-violent civil rights march after Montgomery, and he never did. SNCC was changing in 1965. While Forman was leading the demonstrations in Montgomery, Stokely Carmichael was leading SNCC's efforts in rural Lowndes County. SNCC was organizing the local blacks and forming a political party independent of the local Democratic Party. It was called the Lowndes County Freedom Organization (LCFO), but it became better known as the Black Panther Party. Its symbol was the black panther and the Democratic Party of Alabama's symbol was the white rooster! In 1965, Lowndes County was 80% Black but not a single Black citizen had been able to register to vote. Due to SNCC's efforts by 1966, Blacks ran for county office but failed to win. Willie Ricks, who had organized the students in Montgomery, joined Carmichael in Lowndes County. SNCC had for a long time employed the slogan of 'black power for poor black people' in its organizing efforts. Ricks shortened this slogan to 'Black power' and began using it in his speeches. Ricks, I can attest, was a gifted speaker and could arouse a crowd. "Black power' was getting a good reception in Lowndes County and other places where Ricks spoke. In

June of 1966, after James Meredith had been shot during his March Against Fear, Carmichael started using the slogan Black Power and it caught on nationally.

When Huey P. Newton and Bobby Seale formed the Black Panther Party for Self Defense in 1966 in Oakland, California, they asked the Lowndes County Freedom Organization for permission to use the black panther name for their group. Newton and Seale were originally members of the Revolutionary Action Movement (RAM) that followed the writings of Robert Williams from his exile in Cuba and China. Newton and Seale felt that RAM was not doing enough to confront the violence of the police toward the Black community and formed the Black Panthers.

This shift within SNCC from 'Freedom Now' to 'Black Power' was very significant. People inside and outside the Movement began to conflate Black Power with black nationalism and with black separatism. In turn it was further conflated not just with self-defense, but with retaliatory violence, spontaneous rebellion, and armed struggle. Within SNCC, there was an attempt to replace the leadership of John Lewis with a leadership more favorable to a self-defense, black nationalist agenda. In a contentious election Stokely Carmichael replaced John Lewis as Chairman in 1966. Lewis blamed Forman for undermining his position. Forman denied it, but SNCC took a different direction under Carmichael.

Bill Ware was a SNCC worker in Atlanta's Vine City Project. He was born in Mississippi and went to college at Minnesota. He developed a position paper for the Atlanta Project that laid out the reasons why Whites should be excluded from SNCC. The document made painful reading for me. It is a logical extension of conflating black power with black separatism in that it states that Black people can never have true liberation if Black organizations include Whites.

SNCC had to be "a Black thing" if true Black liberation were to be accomplished. This point of view gathered increasing support within SNCC. Forman was against it originally and Carmichael was initially against it and then acquiesced. Whites were excluded from SNCC in 1966. This included many people like Bob and Dottie Zellner who had risked their lives for SNCC many times.

This also meant that SNCC would not take money from White donors, and this in turn meant that SNCC's funding would soon dry up. Carmichael was a flamboyant, charismatic leader but under his chairmanship SNCC imploded. The organization had gone from a non-violent, inter-racial, militant voice for social change in the South to a self-destructive, Black nationalist, directionless organization that ceased to be any kind of positive factor in American political life.

The seeds for SNCC's self-destruction were sown by Carmichael's interpretation of Black Power, but it was assured beginning in 1968 when H. Rap Brown succeeded Carmichael as Chairman.

Forman eventually left SNCC but never really found a place for his restless intellect and his militancy. In my observation he was always conflicted about his role in the Movement. In Monroe in 1961, he sat on the porch with Robert Williams holding a rifle deep into the night. When the Freedom Riders arrived, he helped organize the non-violent protests and acted as a conduit between Williams and the Freedom Riders. In the SNCC controversies he seemed ambivalent about the issues of White participation, non-violence, and Black nationalism. In the end he sided with the nationalists.

He negotiated an ill-fated joining of SNCC with the Black Panther Party in 1967 and briefly held a position with the Panthers. When SNCC imploded in 1968 and 1969 Forman joined various black radical groups and developed his Black Manifesto. In 1969 he interrupted services at New York's Riverside Church to demand $500 million in reparations from White churches for slavery and other injustices done to Black people. In his later years he earned a Ph.D., wrote several books, and continued to speak about progressive politics and equality. He taught at American University in Washington, DC.

Judge Frank M. Johnson kept on making decisions that helped dismantle segregation in the South piece by piece. In 1966 he ruled that Blacks in Alabama must be permitted to serve on juries. In the same year he ruled that the Alabama poll tax was unconstitutional. In 1970 he ordered that the Montgomery YMCA must be desegregated. Finally, he ruled that the state of Alabama had to hire one black Highway Patrol officer for every White officer hired until parity was reached. Judge Johnson made a significant contribution to the end of segregation in Alabama and the rest of the South with his courageous rulings. These contributions have gone relatively unnoticed in popular histories of the Civil Rights Movement, but they should not be. He received the Presidential Medal of Freedom in 1995.

Dr. Martin Luther King, Jr. led the Selma to Montgomery march, and the media generally gave him credit for the voting effort in Alabama. I was tempted to write that he took credit for the march and all that it represented but that would be too harsh. The media had picked King as the leader of the Civil Rights Movement and his charismatic personality and oratory earned him that position. This also earned him resentment on the part of many SNCC workers. Bernard Lafayette, Jr. and his wife, Colia, began SNCC's voter registration project in Selma in 1963. They were the first civil rights workers in Selma. The Selma march was the idea of Rev. James Bevel of SCLC that by the beginning of 1965 had joined with SNCC for a major push for voting rights in Alabama. And of course, John Lewis was severely beaten on Bloody Sunday. Amelia Boynton was a courageous local leader in Selma. There was plenty of credit to go around, but King was anointed by the media and received most of the credit.

When the Voting Rights Act of 1965 was passed in the summer, Dr. King received the bulk of the credit for that, too. But things were shifting. Dr. King led three major efforts after Selma. The first was the open housing movement in Chicago in 1966. King faced bottle-throwing Whites during marches in Chicago, violence that he said was worse than that he had faced in the South. The second was his opposition to the war in Vietnam. This stand cost him the support of many in the Democratic Party including President Johnson who was having his own significant problems because of the war. Then in 1968 King and SCLC organized the Poor People's Campaign, an effort to address the plight of the nation's poor population relatively unaffected by the civil rights legislation because they were too poor to enjoy its advantages. He was engaged in this effort with sanitation workers in Memphis when he was assassinated in April of 1968.

However, King had lost control of the leadership of the civil right movement long before his death. I have detailed the tensions between SNCC and SCLC before, during, and after the Selma march. James Meredith was the first black person admitted to the University of Mississippi in October of 1962 with the help of Federal marshals, the 2nd Infantry Division, the 503rd Military Police Battalion, and the federalized Mississippi National Guard. In June of 1966, ever his own person, he organized and led a solitary March Against Fear from Memphis to Jackson, Mississippi. When he arrived inside Mississippi, he was immediately shot in the leg. The major civil rights leaders joined the march and vowed to complete it. The NAACP backed out when they learned that the Deacons for Defense and Justice, a self-defense group from Bogalusa, Louisiana were going to provide armed security for the march. It was on this march that Stokely Carmichael, now the

Chairman of SNCC, introduced the slogan 'Black Power.' Dr. King's followers had been using the slogan, 'Freedom Now.' Carmichael told King directly that he wanted to challenge him with the slogan of Black Power and used his presence to use it. King was reported to have replied that he had been used before and that one more time would not hurt. Black Power was a direct challenge to King's philosophy and to his leadership. The differences with SNCC that had been brewing since the difficulties with John Lewis' speech at the March on Washington came out publicly and dramatically on the March Against Fear. Black Power caught on and spread quickly in its appeal.

Factors of difference of approach within the civil rights movement as well as divisions within the liberal-labor coalition over the war in Vietnam, weakened Dr. King's position within the movement and without. The other factor that came into play were the urban insurrections (so-called riots) that began with the Watts Insurrection of the summer of 1965 and continued with similar incidents in Cleveland and Omaha in 1966, Detroit and Newark in 1967, and in Chicago, DC, Baltimore and many other cities in 1968 after Dr. King was murdered. These violent and destructive outbursts can be seen in retrospect as alternatives to the non-violent direct-action approach advocated by Dr. King. Those participating in the insurrections had little stake in the middle-class goals of the Civil Rights Movement and no access to the means of redressing the grievances of police brutality, housing discrimination, lack of job opportunities, and general poverty and decay in the inner cities of the North and West. For these people, Jim Forman's alternative of 'knocking the fucking legs off" of the table of democracy seemed the only viable alternative.

In the summer of 1966 with members of Ann Arbor CORE, I saw Dr. King give a speech in the middle of 12th Street in Detroit Dr. King had come to Detroit as part of his campaign in Chicago for open

101

housing. My grandfather used to take me to a deli on 12th Street when I was little for a corned beef sandwich and "red pop" that was my favorite drink. Dr. King was greeted by a large and enthusiastic group of mostly young people in the middle of a warm weekday. I told my friend from CORE that I thought that this was going to be the location where a "riot" could occur. Sure enough, the following summer a raid on a blind pig on 12th Street and Clairmount set off four days of civil disturbance in which 43 people were killed, 1189 injured, 7200 arrested, and countless businesses destroyed by fire.

One result of the urban insurrections is that they tended to polarize both the Black and White communities, both locally and nationally. Radicals on both sides were seen as offering solutions that moderates could not. This was leaving Dr. King and the non-violent movement weaker and less influential.

The major players in the Montgomery drama continued to influence the civil rights movements in these varied ways. As for us, the minor players, we went our own ways. Rory and Jim went South again in the summer to Bogalusa, Louisiana where the Deacons for Defense and Justice were waging a campaign for human rights while advocating armed self-defense. They both became social psychology professors. I never went to the South again. I worked with the NAACP in Willow Run near Ann Arbor on housing and job discrimination. Willow Run was the site of the largest bomber plant in the world during World War II. It brought Black and White workers from the South to work in the plant, and they stayed on as the plant was turned to automobile manufacturing after the war. Racial discrimination in housing and jobs continued into the sixties.

I received my Ph.D. in clinical psychology, married, and was flying to my first job at UCLA in 1969. The day my pregnant wife and I were flying to Los Angeles, Robert Williams was flying back to the

United States and was due to arrive in Detroit as we were leaving. By this time, Williams had been elected president of a group called the Republic of New Afrika. This was a Black nationalist group that demanded land in the South for the establishment of a self-sustaining Black republic. Uniformed young men ringed the airport terminal and were stationed at strategic points on the roof. On our way to our gate, we saw Mabel Williams, Robert's wife, and one young son waiting for her husband's arrival alone in a room. I wondered if I should go talk to her. After all I had stayed in her house. However, I decided against it, and we made our way to our gate and to my first job as a psychology professor in California.

Additional Reading

Curtis J. Austin (2006). *Up Against the Wall: Violence in the Making and Unmaking of the Black Panther Party.* Fayetteville: University of Arkansas Press.

Stokely Carmichael and Charles Hamilton (1967). *Black Power: The Politics of Liberation.* New York: Vintage

David Garrow (1986). *Bearing the Cross: Martin Luther King, Jr., and the Southern Christian Leadership Conference.* New York: William Morrow.

Jeffrey Ogbor (2004). *Black Power: Radical Politics and African American Identity.* Baltimore: Johns Hopkins University Press.

Photo 28: White Citizens Council sign on State Highway 80 between Selma and Montgomery. (Image from the Glen Pearcy Collection, courtesy of the American Folklife Center, Library of Congress, afc 2012040_059_16)

Photo 29: The White counter-protest march, Montgomery, March 18, 1965. (Image from the Glen Pearcy Collection, courtesy of the American Folklife Center, Library of Congress, afc 2012040_060_07)

Photo 30: White counter-protest march, Montgomery. (Image from the Glen Pearcy Collection, courtesy of the American Folklife Center, Library of Congress, afc 2012040_060_11)

Photo 31: White counter-protest march, Montgomery. (Image from the Glen Pearcy Collection, courtesy of the American Folklife Center, Library of Congress, afc 2012040_060_17)

Photo 32: White counter-protest march, Montgomery. (Image from the Glen Pearcy Collection, courtesy of the American Folklife Center, Library of Congress, afc 2012040_061_07)

Photo 33: White counter-protest march, Montgomery. (Image from the Glen Pearcy Collection, courtesy of the American Folklife Center, Library of Congress, afc 2012040_061_19)

106

Photo 34: White counter-protest march, Montgomery. (Image from the Glen Pearcy Collection, courtesy of the American Folklife Center, Library of Congress, afc 2012040_061_04)

Photo 35: White counter-protest march, Montgomery. (Image from the Glen Pearcy Collection, courtesy of the American Folklife Center, Library of Congress, afc 2012040_061_03)

Chapter VII

Re-Appraisal: 60 Years On: The White Backlash

"Backlash Blues" written by Langston Hughes and sung by Nina Simone:

Mister Backlash, Mister Backlash,
Just who do think I am?
You raise my taxes, freeze my wages,
Send my son to Vietnam.

You give me second class houses,
Second class schools,
Do you think colored folks
Are just second-class fools?

When I try to find a job
To earn a little cash, All you got to offer
Is a white backlash.

But the world is big,
Big and bright and round –
And it full of folks like me who are
Black, Yellow, Beige, and Brown.

Mister Backlash, Mister Backlash,
What do you think I got to lose?
I'm going to leave, you, Mister Backlash
Singing your mean old backlash blues.

You're the one
Will have the blues,
Not me –
Wait and see!

It has been almost 60 years since the Selma-Montgomery Campaign ended, plenty of time to reflect on the accomplishments and disappointments of this phase of the Civil Rights Movement. The entire Selma Campaign, including the Montgomery marches, contributed to the passage of the Voting Rights Act in the summer of 1965. Lyndon Johnson had to be pushed to fully support a voting rights bill, but he eventually did on the night we marchers were surrounded by Alabama state troopers. He gathered bi-partisan support in Congress and the support of the American people outside of the White South. The Selma-Montgomery marches were the high watermark of the non-violent student movement. State-supported segregation was being dismantled.

As I will discuss, two other trends were in the works as well. The student-labor -liberal -religious coalition was about to break apart. SNCC in particular was to change leadership and philosophy and by the end of 1966 was a different kind of organization. The other trend was one I have documented with pictures of the White people's protest march in Montgomery on the day we left. The signs suggest the beginning of what has become the narrative of White Grievance by which the granting of fundamental civil rights to Blacks means the diminution of rights of Whites. This narrative reflects the kind of zero sum thinking that pervades the political discussion today.

The cost of Johnson's all-out support for civil rights was the loss of White Southern voters to the Republican Party. This White exodus from the Democratic Party can be seen to have begun when Johnson uttered the words, 'We SHALL overcome,' in his speech to Congress when we were surrounded by the Alabama Highway Patrol in Montgomery. Johnson had joined the cause of civil rights, and this is the reason that legislatures and governors are Republican in the South today. In the minds of white southerners, Johnson had stuck a dagger in the heart of Dixie that night as the mayor of Selma aptly put it.

The Selma campaign also highlighted the growing rift between SNCC and Dr. King's SCLC. Stokely Carmichael, soon to unseat John Lewis as Chairman of SNCC, did join Dr. King when the Selma March came through Lowndes County, but Jim Forman did not. The Montgomery marches were bi-racial and non-violent, but the seeds for black nationalism and armed self-defense were already at work in SNCC. The rift would widen in the next year with the march in support of James Meredith and when whites were excluded from SNCC, both of which occurred in 1966. In retrospect, the Selma campaign was SNCC's last participation in the Civil Rights Movement. By the next year SNCC had turned to the Black Power Movement.

The reasons for the collapse of the Civil Rights Coalition are many, and there is plenty of blame to go around. The reasons include the disillusionment with the Democratic Party over the seating of the

Mississippi Freedom Democratic Party during the 1964 Democratic convention, the radicalization of white and black activists, the urban insurrections (riots) beginning with Watts in 1965, the anti-Vietnam War Movement, the assassinations, and the White Backlash. In this sense, if the Civil Rights Movement was the Second Reconstruction, it ended in much the same way as the First Reconstruction. That is, the efforts to undo the effects of slavery, segregation, and discrimination fell short of its goal and allowed the forces of the White Backlash to regain strength and try to turn back all that had been accomplished.

SNCC and CORE had been working since 1961 to establish a grass-roots movement in Mississippi. The 'freedom summer' of 1964 was but one phase of this effort to encourage indigenous leadership to fight for civil rights, especially the right to vote, in the face of an entrenched violent white supremacist network in Mississippi. This effort resulted in the Mississippi Freedom Democratic Party that sent a delegation to the 1964 Democratic Convention. They had hoped to unseat the White segregationist Mississippi delegation to the convention. They pointed out that the segregationists were elected by an illegal vote in which Blacks, 40% of Mississippi's population, were excluded from voting and that the segregationists had no intention of supporting Lyndon Johnson for president. The credentials committee televised the hearings at which MFDP workers like Fannie Lou Hamer and Aaron Henry spoke. President Johnson tried to prevent Hamer's appearance. In the end, delegates from other southern states threatened a walk-out if the MFDP was seated as the rightful delegation from Mississippi. Johnson, fearful of losing the upcoming election against Barry Goldwater, capitulated to this maneuver. Led by Hubert Humphrey and Walter Mondale, the Democratic Party offered a "compromise": the MFDP would have 2 delegates who act as observers and the segregationist delegation would be seated. This "compromise" was rejected, but the damage was done.

The state of Mississippi voted for Barry Goldwater and has never voted for another Democratic candidate for president to this day (1976 and Jimmy Carter was the only exception). The civil rights activists were deeply disillusioned by the actions of President Johnson, Hubert Humphrey, Walter Mondale, and the rest of the Democratic Party establishment. This was the Compromise of 1877 all over again. This was a major blow to the Civil Rights Movement, a major mistake by the Democratic Party, and possibly factor in the frustrations leading to the urban insurrections and the turn to the Black Power Movement.

After a talk I gave to high schoolers in the South Bronx in 2015 about the events I have described in earlier chapters, I was told by one young man that the Civil Rights Movement really did not change anything because it was not "revolutionary" as Malcolm X had advocated. From the vantage point of the South Bronx, one of the nation's most segregated school systems, the young man may have had a point. On the other hand, many White Americans believed in 2015 that because of the Civil Rights Movement we lived in a color-blind society where everyone has a fair chance. I do not agree with either of these conclusions. My own view is that the Civil Rights Movement dismantled state-sponsored segregation in the South and partially addressed racial discrimination in housing, education, employment, and economic opportunity in the country as a whole. This constituted a revolutionary change in a comparatively short period of time, particularly in the South. On the other hand, the economic goals of the Movement, particularly addressing the needs of the underclass in our cities have fallen far short, and as a result we have seen some of the other gains in public, education, voting rights, and criminal justice erode and move backwards. The issues of systemic racism and White supremacist attitudes were not fully understood or addressed at all.

Among the many reasons for the break-up of the Civil Rights Coalition, the White Backlash is certainly a factor that continues to play a part in our politics to this day.

In discussing the White Backlash to the Civil Rights Movement, I would like to begin with a brief discussion of the First Reconstruction from 1865 to 1877. The reader will recall that after the Civil War the Republican Party of Abraham Lincoln sought to grant citizenship rights to the freed enslaved and this included the right to vote for Black men. Women of all races were not given the right to vote until 1920.

A Civil Rights Act was proposed in 1865 and vetoed by President Andrew Johnson, a Democrat. It was passed in 1866. The 14th and 15 Amendments to the Constitution guaranteed equal rights for Black former slaves and legislation and federal agencies were created to guarantee these rights would be realized. General William Sherman issued his famous Special Field Order Number 15, distributing 400,000 acres of land in 40-acre parcels to freed enslaved in coastal South Carolina, Georgia, and north-central Florida. President Andrew Johnson cancelled this order before its program could be widely implemented. Today, the community of Royal, Florida has Black families with 40-acre parcels that were received as a result of Sherman's land re-distribution plan during Reconstruction. A Freedman's Bureau was set up, and another Civil Rights Act was passed in 1875 that guaranteed non-discrimination in public accommodations. The Justice Department was established in 1870 in large part to fight the Ku Klux Klan that had become the terrorist paramilitary wing of the Democrat Party in the South. Legislation in 1870 and 1871 gave President Grant the authority to battle the Klan that was fighting a guerilla war against Reconstruction. Blacks voted in large numbers in the elections of 1868, 1872, and 1876. It is important to note that Black rights were enforced by federal troops in the former Confederate states while Whites loyal to the Confederacy fought Reconstruction tooth and nail.

In the presidential election of 1876, the Democrat Samuel Tilden won the popular vote but there was a challenge in the Electoral College. The votes of three former Confederate States (Louisiana, Florida, and South Carolina) were challenged by both parties. Without these states Tilden was one vote short of election, and with these states the Republican, Rutherford B. Hayes, would win the election in the Electoral College. A 15-person Electoral Commission was appointed and Hayes was declared the winner by an 8-7 vote along party lines. Further a deal was apparently made in the Congress, whereby Hayes would be declared President and he would agree to withdraw federal troops from the former Confederate states.

This came to be known as the Compromise of 1877. It stopped the First Reconstruction in its tracks, and it paved the way for Jim Crow laws and the system of state-sponsored segregation. The Civil Rights Act of 1875 was declared unconstitutional by the Supreme Court in 1883. In 1896 the case of Plessy v. Ferguson upheld the constitutionality of Louisiana's segregation law in public transportation. The factors behind the failure of the First Reconstruction to secure the rights of the freed enslaved was a combination of a vicious White backlash on the part of White Southerners and a capitulation on the part of White Northerners to letting the South deal with the freed enslaved and their descendants through a cruel social and economic system. It was a disgraceful chapter in the country's history as exploitative share-cropping replaced slavery, and black disenfranchisement took place through intimidation, violence, and a tangled system of poll taxes, literacy, tests, and the individual whims of White registrars. The system of segregation was rigidly enforced through state law as well as extra-judicial violence in the form of at least 5,000 racial lynchings between the years 1877 and 1950.

One of the consequences of the failure of Reconstruction to secure the rights guaranteed by the Constitution was the Great Migration of Blacks from the South to cities in the North, Midwest, and West. Between 1910 and 1970, 6.6 million blacks moved from the South to cities like New York, Philadelphia, Cleveland, Detroit, Chicago, and Los Angeles to escape the violence of segregation and to seek better economic opportunities. In 1910 about 90% of America's Black community lived in the South and by 1970 that figure had dropped in half. The greatest exodus came from Mississippi, Louisiana, Alabama, and Georgia. We are still dealing with the effects of the Great Migration today in our northern and western cities. But it goes back to the White backlash against Reconstruction!

The Civil Rights Movement then had to address many of the same issues that the First Reconstruction sought to deal with: public accommodations, economic discrimination, and voting rights. However, it also had to deal with the new system of segregation with its own state laws and paramilitary violence in the revived Ku Klux Klan. It was *déjà vu* all over again and then some.

However, don't let anyone tell you that the Civil Rights Movement didn't accomplish anything. The break-up of state sponsored segregation was the greatest achievement that any social movement has accomplished non-violently in the history of the United States and perhaps the world.

In addition, the Civil Rights Movement enabled other groups to mount successful movements on behalf of other minorities in the United States. The success of the Feminist Movement, the LGBT Movement, the Individuals with Disabilities Movement owes a good deal to the civil rights folks of 1955 to 1968. It was not until 1989 that I realized that maybe the civil rights movement had really had an impact. The image of a lone Chinese student confronting a line of tanks in Tiananmen Square in Beijing, China became an image that will forever represent the confrontation between the individual and authoritarian dictatorship. When American reporters asked the Chinese students who participated in the uprising in 1989 what sparked this mode of protest, the students replied that they were inspired by the American students of the 1960's who confronted segregation in a non-violent way. I was stunned when I heard this. After so much that had happened this seemed to be the best indication that we really did make a difference. It was ironic that Robert Williams and the Black Panthers were looking to Mao for a guide to dealing with racism in the United States, and the Chinese students were looking to the non-violent Civil Rights Movement for inspiration in protesting the excesses of Chinese Communist authoritarianism!

The Voting Rights Act of 1965 with its sections 4 and 5 enforcement brought Blacks into political office all over the South. Selma has a Black congresswoman, a Black mayor, and a majority Black city council. John Lewis became the dean of the Georgia Congressional delegation and was dubbed the "conscience of the Congress." Needless to say, Barak Obama was elected president twice! The link between the Alabama Voting registration movement centered in Selma and the passage of the Voting Rights Act is clear.

There was a revolution in the South that brought down the system of state-supported segregation and that revolution inspired other movements and brought awareness of the concept of human rights. There is much to cheer and much to be proud of. So much for the good news.

The election of 1968 can be viewed as the end point of the Second Reconstruction just as the election of 1876 was the end of the first.

Richard Nixon with his "Southern Strategy" and his appeal to "Law and Order" was able to appeal to the White Backlash and set in motion a white Republican take-over of the South and much of the country. The political far-Left bears some responsibility for this turn of events. The turn to violence, to unrealistic ideology on the part of the student movement and the Black Power Movement only provided fuel for the backlash. The urban insurrections and the Vietnam War fractured the religious-labor-student coalition that had won over a majority of well-meaning Americans to the cause of Civil Rights. The assassinations of Dr. King and Bobby Kennedy in 1968 took a huge toll as well. Just as in 1876 the country was unable or unwilling to sustain the gains made by the movement for human rights and turned to backlash.

White resistance to voting rights began almost as soon as the Voting Rights Act of 1965 was signed. This resistance came to be centered in two prominent places: the Senate office of one Jesse Helms of North Carolina and the Supreme Court office of Chief Justice William Rehnquist.

Jesse Helms was elected to the Senate in 1972 and became the longest serving elected United States senator in North Carolina history. He was an arch-Conservative, an early supporter of Ronald Reagan, and an outspoken racist. He was also an obstructionist, fighting civil rights, disability rights, abortion rights, feminism, affirmative action, and even the National Endowment for the Arts. He became known as 'Senator No.' He was opposed to the Voting Rights Act of 1965 in particular and sought to use his office to undermine it in any way he could. Helms was born in, of all places, Monroe, Union County, North Carolina, the home also of Robert F. Williams, the outspoken NAACP leader I have described earlier. Senator Helms was named after his father, "Big Jesse" Helms. Big Jesse served as both police chief and fire chief in Monroe. He was fire chief when I visited Monroe in 1961.

In his autobiography Robert Williams recalled as a child seeing Big Jesse dragging a Black woman off to jail by her hair. Williams asserted that the Monroe police and fire departments had many Klan members in them during Big Jesse's time. Beginning in 1972, Little Jesse's Senate office was the headquarters for efforts to obstruct and undo the Voting Rights Act of 1965. This effort continued in North Carolina even after Helms' retirement from the Senate in 2003.

The second major center of opposition to the Voting Rights Act of 1965 was centered in the office of then Associate Supreme Court Justice William H. Rehnquist. Nixon's re-election in 1972 enabled him to appoint Rehnquist to replace Justice John Harlan. Harlan, though a conservative on the Warren court, generally had supported desegregation and civil rights efforts. Reagan's election gave the opportunity for the President to appoint Rehnquist Chief Justice in 1986 , and he served until 2005. In 1952, Rehnquist had worked as a law clerk for Supreme Court Justice Robert H. Jackson. Rehnquist wrote a memorandum against court-ordered school desegregation while the Court was deciding the famous Brown v. Topeka Board of Education school desegregation case. Rehnquist argued that the separate but equal doctrine of Plessey v. Ferguson ought to be upheld, and further argued that the majority had the right to determine what the rights of a minority ought to be. The Brown case was decided in 1954 and the majority of the Court rejected Rehnquist's argument. Desegregation of the schools was determined to be the law of the land although it took a mighty struggle to try to implement that law. In his confirmation hearings in 1971, Rehnquist sought to attribute his memo to Jackson's views rather than his own. Fellow law clerks, however, testified that Rehnquist had argued with them against desegregation. Still, he was confirmed, and his office became a center of opposition to Black voting rights.

In his 1986 confirmation hearing for Chief Justice, Rehnquist was accused of intimidating black voters in Phoenix in 1962. Rehnquist was a supporter of conservative Barry Goldwater and urged Goldwater to oppose the Civil Rights Act of 1964. A witness to the intimidation of Black voters, psychologist Sydney Smith, testified that he saw Rehnquist harassing black voters. By coincidence I met Syd Smith in 1969 when I visited the Menninger Foundation in Topeka where he worked as a respected psychologist and psychoanalyst. I never knew about this aspect of his life until I was researching this chapter.

In 1980, a young Harvard Law School graduate named John Roberts served as a law clerk for Justice Rehnquist when the justice's office was a center for conservative legal efforts to reverse the liberal decisions of the 1950's and 1960's. In 1980 the Supreme Court sided with Mobile, Alabama and ruled that voting rights cases had to prove "discriminatory motivation," something that was not part of the original Voting Rights Act of 1965 and something very hard to prove. This case helped shaped Roberts' views of civil rights and he sought to continue Rehnquist's agenda to roll back civil rights legislation, a legal backlash.

In 2005 John G. Roberts was appointed by President George W. Bush to be Chief Justice of the Supreme Court, succeeding William Rehnquist. In the 2013 case, Shelby County v. Holder. the Court in a 5-4 decision gutted the enforcement provisions of the Voting Rights Act. This was the culmination of decades of the opposition of Rehnquist and Roberts to the law. Roberts penned the majority decision and argued that Federal oversight in jurisdictions mostly in the South were outdated, unnecessary, and unjustified. Almost immediately after the Roberts ruling, two states, Texas, and North Carolina, passed state legislation aimed at making it harder for Blacks to vote. The Texas law required a driver's license or a gun license in order to vote.

North Carolina imposed a strict ID requirement on voters, limited times for registration, and restricted early voting times often used by Black voters. Georgia then passed legislation changing the dates of elections in municipalities with high Black populations from November to May in an attempt to suppress Black voter turn-out. Alabama then instituted a strict ID requirement for voting and then shut down offices that issued driver's licenses in every predominantly Black county.

Roberts' assessment that the enforcement sections of the Voting Rights Act were no longer necessary was not only wrong but seemed to be motivated by his long-standing effort along with William Rehnquist and Jesse Helms to undo the gains of the Civil Rights Movement and the promise of Black suffrage begun during the first Reconstruction. This assault on the Voting Rights Act's enforcement provisions, became the equivalent of withdrawing Federal troops after the first Reconstruction. The withdrawal of troops led eventually to the system of segregation and the disenfranchisement of Black voters. Without the threat of federal enforcement, states began to implement ways of suppressing the Black vote once again.

Alabama today is a case in point. After the Compromise of 1876, the suppression of Black voting was accomplished by the following means: poll taxes, literacy tests, "grandfather" clauses, discriminatory election procedures, black codes and segregation laws, gerrymandering, white-only primaries, eligibility requirements, and the re-writing of state constitutions. This system of voter suppression was enforced with physical intimidation and lynching. This was the system we faced in 1965 when we went to Montgomery to march for voting rights. This system of voter suppression and segregation was undone by the Voting Rights Act of 1965 and it increased Black enfranchisement. Then came Mr. Backlash and the slow undoing of progress in civil rights.

In the election of 2016, black voter suppression was certainly present but in more sophisticated form. The tools at the disposal of the by now Republican White majority in Alabama consists of a few of the old methods plus some new features.

The means used in the 2016 election to suppress black voting included election procedures, gerrymandering, and eligibility requirements. The Republican-majority legislature in 2011 passed new voting restrictions that went into effect for the 2012 election without Federal approval. The case that allowed the Roberts Court to gut the enforcement provisions of the Voting Rights Act came from Shelby County in Alabama. Shelby County, 90% White and 80% Republican, sued the Federal government asserting that the enforcement sections (4 and 5) of the Voting Rights Act were unconstitutional on the basis that the "climate" that had produced the act in 1965 was no longer applicable in 2013. The John Roberts Supreme Court agreed.

The 2013 Shelby County case reinforced the voter restriction laws passed in 2011, but the strict voter ID regulations were followed after the Shelby case by the closing of 31 Department of Motor Vehicle locations where IDs were issued. DMV offices were closed in 8 of the 10 counties with the highest concentrations of black voters. Selma still has a DMV office but most of the surrounding Black Belt counties do not. It was estimated that 250,000 registered voters in Alabama do not have a driver's license or other government-issued identification card. Only 41% of eligible Alabamians voted in 2016, the lowest turn-out in 30 years. Alabama ranked last in voter access in a recent survey.

Another voter suppression mechanism used by white Alabamians has been the effort to gerrymander voting districts in the state in such a way as to give advantage to white Republican candidates for state and local office. This has been a cynical and clever long-range plan to blunt Black voting power while seeming to adhere to voting rights principles.

For example, there are 7 Congressional districts in Alabama. The Black population of the state is about 26% but Black residents are not evenly distributed across the state. In 2012, the Republican legislature passed a re-districting plan that placed the Black Belt counties plus the Black neighborhoods of Montgomery, Birmingham, and Tuscaloosa (where the University of Alabama is located) into one Congressional district, the 7th. This made for a predominantly Black voting district which could and did elect a black Congresswoman, Terri Sewall from Selma.

However, the effect of this plan was to reduce the chances of districts in which there could be a competitive Democrat-Republican contest. Further, it had the effect of reducing the influence of White Democrats and racializing the political parties. In Alabama the Republican Party is almost exclusively White and the Democrat Party is increasingly Black but marginalized.

If one looks at a map of the Alabama 7th District, it is a funny-looking odd shape that has no logical borders. It extends into the Black neighborhoods of Montgomery and Birmingham but also into Tuscaloosa like a misshapen amoeba.

The only reason for such an arrangement is to put as many Black voters into it as possible. The other 6 districts are predominantly White and are represented by six White Republicans. The intent of these gerrymanders, what Jesse Jackson called "stacking and packing," has been to reduce the potential power of Black voting and to reduce the influence of Black and White Democrats working together. This has successfully solidified White Republican power in Alabama. This strategy has been largely successful and other states, including some in the North, have followed this strategy as well.

In 2015, the Supreme Court ruled in Alabama Black Caucus v. Alabama that the state's re-districting legislative plan was "racially motivated" and illegal. Racial quotas were found to have been used in each district to appear to comply with the Voting Rights Act by keeping majority Black districts intact. In the wake of this ruling the Alabama legislature altered slightly the district boundaries but essentially keep to the gerrymandering strategy that had been successful in the past. The Supreme Court decision was specific to the boundaries of certain Alabama districts but did not address the more general issue of Republican racial gerrymandering.

However, in June of 2023 even the Supreme Court had had enough of the obvious racial gerrymandering and ordered the Alabama legislature to redraw its congressional districts map. The legislature did so, but a lower court ruling was that the legislature did not comply with the court's intentions to draw a second district in which a competitive contest would be possible. At this writing, the legislature is appealing.

The other tool used to suppress the Black vote in Alabama as well as other states has been felon disenfranchisement laws. Alabama's law went back to 1901 when the state passed a new constitution stripping voting rights from anyone who had committed a crime of "moral turpitude," leaving the interpretation of that concept ambiguous. However, the intent of this law was made clear by the White president of the constitutional convention. He declared that the purpose of the law was to "establish white supremacy" in Alabama. The law and its motivation resulted in purging Blacks from the voter rolls and this law continued to have this effect until 2018.

It might be thought that laws preventing convicted felons from voting goes back the founding of the country. In fact, these laws were passed only after the first Reconstruction and were largely designed to prevent Blacks from voting. Kentucky, Florida, and Iowa had mandated permanent disenfranchisement for all people with felony convictions. Florida recently passed a citizen-initiated amendment to the state constitution allowing the reinstatement of voting rights except in convictions for murder and sexual crimes. However, the Republican legislature, ignoring the will of the people, passed legislation making it more difficult for felons to have their voting rights restored by instituting what amounts to a poll tax for convicted felons.

Tennessee, Mississippi, Delaware, Wyoming, Arizona, and Nevada disenfranchise some people with criminal convictions. Vermont and New Hampshire have no disenfranchisement of felons and the rest of the states have voting rights restored after release from prison or after parole and probation.

We can see that the states treat this issue very differently. Particularly in the South, these felon disenfranchisement laws were instituted after Reconstruction as part of the effort to prevent Blacks from voting in significant numbers. In Alabama this was made explicit. In 1985, the Supreme Court ruled that the "moral turpitude" Provision of Alabama's law was a violation of the equal protection clause of the Constitution, but it was reinstated 11 years later by the Alabama legislature. The law was finally changed in 2018. However, government officials decided that the state would not inform the former felons that their voting rights were restored! It is thought that this affected as many as 250,000 voters in the state, most of them Black.

A 2023 study by Marco Tabellini at the Harvard Business School and his colleagues demonstrated that the Voting Rights Act of 1965 triggered "significant and long-lasting" opposition among the White population of the Southern states most affected by the law. Their county-by-county analysis showed that where the effects of the law were strongest, these areas displayed more negative racial attitudes including more racially-motivated hate crimes by Whites against Blacks.

This study demonstrates the effects of the backlash. This study also calls attention to the zero-sum thinking that I have mentioned also as part of the narrative of White grievance. Granting fundamental rights to one group does not mean the automatic diminution of the rights of another group. Power can be shared.

I have tried to trace an overview of the struggle to achieve the goal of one person/one vote in the state of Alabama from 1965 to the present. It seems that we are still in the period of backlash from the gains of the Civil Rights Movement. The Ku Klux Klan is much less in evidence than in 1965 and Alabama is no longer a terrorist state. However, the struggle continues as techniques like gerrymandering, felon disenfranchisement, voter identification laws, and the like are designed to suppress the Black vote and promote White political supremacy.

I have also focused almost exclusively on the matter of voting rights. Questions of Black-White income and net worth disparity, re-segregation in education, criminal justice, affordable housing, extra-judicial racial police shootings, and the achievement gap in schools all deserve close attention and can be as pressing as the voting issue.

Am I discouraged by the extent of the White Backlash since 1965? I am disappointed to be sure and dismayed to see chanting Nazis march in Charlottesville, Virginia and have a President elected in 2016 and running again in 2024 who believes in White supremacy. I am not discouraged, however. The quest for freedom is a constant struggle as the saying goes. Each generation struggles to make things just a little bit better. The same forces that we faced in Montgomery in 1965 are still around but in a different guise and using different methods.

We need a Third Reconstruction. Rev. William Barber II, the head of the NAACP in North Carolina has outlined a coalition that can make up a movement for justice that will be able to fulfill the unfinished tasks of the previous Reconstructions. Whether Barber's vision will be the one that comes to fruition or whether a different one will come along is hard to say. What is certain is the universal right to vote in Alabama and the rest of the country is the key to achieving the kind of community that so many have worked for so long to achieve. As John Lewis was fond of saying, we have to keep the faith and keep on keeping on!

Additional Reading

Michelle Alexander (2010). *The New Jim Crow: Mass Incarceration in The Age of Colorblindness.* New York: The New Press.

William J. Barber II & Jonathan Wilson-Hartgrove (2016). *The Third Reconstruction: Moral Mondays, Fusion Politics, and the Rise of a New Justice Movement.* Boston: Beacon Press.

W.E.B. DuBois (1935). *Black Reconstruction.* Harcourt, Brace.Thomas Edsall (2013) Keeping Black Voters in Their Place. *New York Times.* November 5, 2013.

Henry Louis Gates, Jr. (2019). *Stony the Road: Reconstruction, White Supremacy, and the Rise of Jim Crow.* New York: Penguin Press.

Thomas Piketty (2013) [2014]. *Capital in the 21st Century.* Cambridge, MA:Belknap Press.

Photo 36: 50th anniversary of Bloody Sunday at the Edmund Pettus Bridge, Selma, Alabama, 2015

Acknowledgments

This book was a long time in the making mostly because I was not sure that anyone other than my family would be interested in my recollections. There are people to thank, however, as this project comes to fruition.

I wish first to acknowledge the people of the High Street/Jackson Avenue neighborhood of Montgomery, Alabama who housed and fed us for a week of great turmoil, endangering themselves in the process. I am grateful to the man who moved his family and stayed up all night on his porch with a rifle and shotgun while we slept after our lives were directly threatened.

My fellow University of Michigan students, Norm Hatter, Hank Kaufmann, Jim Ledvinka, Rory O'Day, and the late Charles Tyler turned out to be good travel companions who bonded as foot soldiers in a non-violent army.

I was surprised over the years to see the amount of photographic evidence of the events I describe in this book. I had the photos that Norm Hatter took, and I thank him for allowing me to use the one he took of John Lewis, just out of the hospital after the beating he took on Bloody Sunday.

I wish also to acknowledge the Jack Rabin Collection of the Penn State University Library for permission to use several images that apparently were originally taken by the Subversive Unit of the Investigative and Identification Division of the Alabama Department of Public Safety.

I wish also to thank Guha Shankar, Folklore Specialist in the American Folklife Center and Co-Director of the Civil Rights History Project Library of Congress. He arranged permission for me to use photos from the extensive Glen Pearcy Collection in the Library of Congress. Glen Pearcy was a student photographer for the *Harvard Crimson* who covered the demonstrations in Selma and Montgomery. His photos tell the story of the demonstrations in ways that words cannot. We overlapped at Harvard, but I never knew him. The experience in Montgomery led him and his wife to work in southwest Georgia for many years.

Bruce Hartford of the Civil Rights Movement Archives provided me with a great deal of useful information about photographs and their copyrights. He was himself in Montgomery and Selma with the SCLC.

I am most grateful to International Psychoanalytic Books (IPBooks) and its Editor-in-Chief Arnold D. Richards, himself a civil rights veteran. The staff of IPBooks, especially Tamar Schwartz and Lawrence Schwartz, were supportive and easy to work with.

I thank my three children who read the manuscript at various stages and made criticisms and suggestions. Two of them were able to join me and my wife in Selma for the 50th anniversary of the Bloody Sunday march to the Edmund Pettus Bridge.

Washington, DC, 2024

www.ingramcontent.com/pod-product-compliance
Lightning Source LLC
Chambersburg PA
CBHW071006120626
46546CB00003B/954